AIRPLANES

AIRPLANES

Written by Moira Butterfield • Illustrated by Mark Bergin

First edition for the United States,
its territories, dependencies, Canada,
and the Philippine Islands, published
1999 by Barron's Educational Series, Inc.

Art Director Robert Walster
Editor-in-Chief John C. Miles
Consultant Andrew Nahum

First published in 1999 by Franklin Watts, London
96 Leonard Street, London EC2A 4XD

All inquiries should be addressed to:
Barron's Educational Series, Inc.
250 Wireless Boulevard
Hauppauge, NY 11788
http://www.barronseduc.com

Library of Congress Catalog Card No. 98-74907
International Standard Book No. 0-7641-5194-0

Printed in Hong Kong

9 8 7 6 5 4 3 2 1

CONTENTS

INTRODUCTION

THE REMARKABLE AIRPLANES IN THIS BOOK are all very different from each other. The very first one was an awkward shaky-looking thing glued together from pieces of wood, fabric, and wire.
It hardly got off the ground, and soon after its first flight a gust of wind nearly blew it to bits. Now the most modern airplanes are sleek and mean, like space-age machines from a science-fiction film. They fly so high and so fast that this book is probably the closest look at them you'll ever get.

▲ A Wright biplane, early 1900s

▲ Alcock and Brown land in Ireland, 1919

Despite seeming so different, all the airplanes chosen here have one thing in common - they were the very best of their time. That is how they made their mark on flying history. Their designers, mechanics, and pilots were pretty special, too. Without them these machines would have never performed the way that they did.

The early pilots flew with unbelievable bravery. Nearly frozen from the weather and often guessing at their position, they needed lots of luck to make it through the trip. The wartime fighter pilots rode

▲ P-51D Mustang, 1943

into battle like brave horsemen of another era, fighting one-to-one for their lives, while modern pilots do seemingly impossible stunts at supersonic, super-scary speeds.

So sit back, fasten your seatbelt, and come along for a ride with the very best.

▲ Charles Lindbergh's *Spirit of St. Louis*, 1927

WRIGHT "FLYER"

Sunday, December 17, 1903 was an extraordinary day in human history. On the coast of North Carolina, near a place called Kitty Hawk, brothers Wilbur and Orville Wright tried out their new flying machine. It flew for 120 ft (36.5 m), the world's first powered, controlled manned flight. Later that day, Wilbur flew 852 ft (260 m).

▲ Wilbur (left) and Orville Wright. They ran a bicycle factory and shop in Dayton, Ohio, before experimenting with flight.

▶ The Wrights' airplane was launched from a miniature railway track.

▲ The plane was controlled by "wing warping." Cables attached to the wings twisted the edges up or down. This, in combination with the use of the aircraft's rudder and elevators, made the plane turn, rise, or dive.

The Wrights didn't work everything out entirely on their own. British engineer George Cayley discovered how wings worked. German Otto Lilienthal designed and flew gliders, and French-American Octave Chanute first designed a biplane. He gave the brothers his expert advice, support, and encouragement.

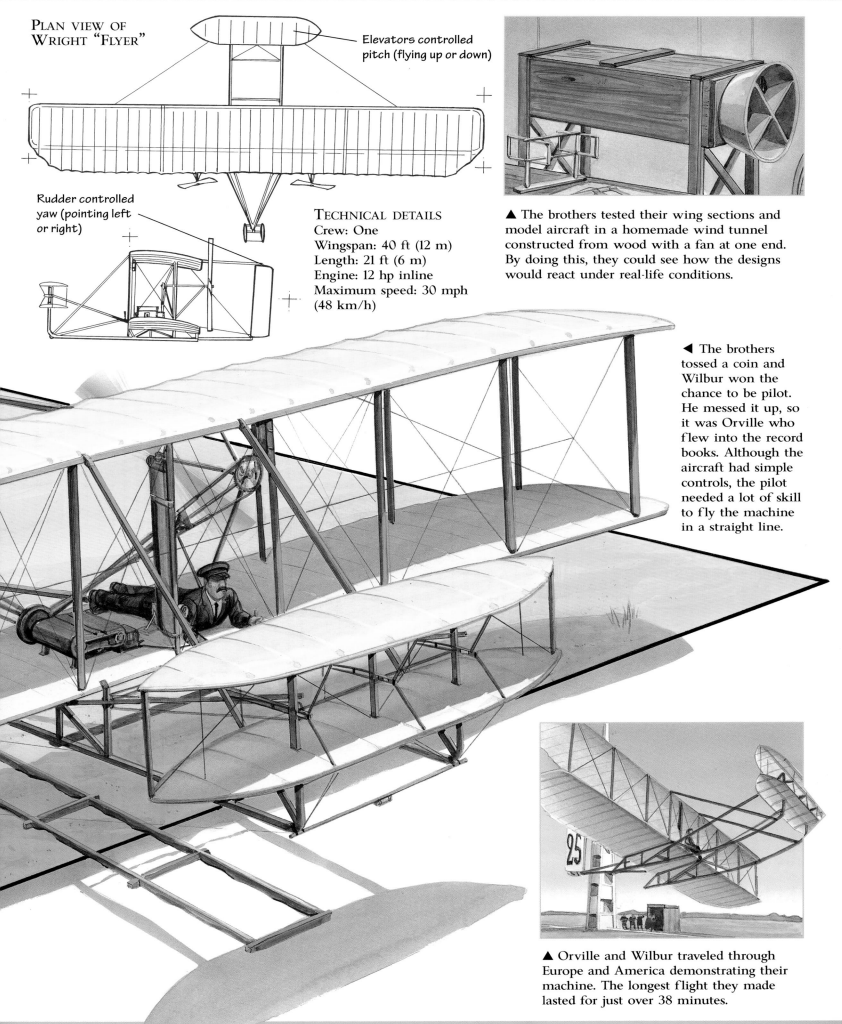

PLAN VIEW OF
WRIGHT "FLYER"

Elevators controlled
pitch (flying up or down)

Rudder controlled
yaw (pointing left
or right)

TECHNICAL DETAILS
Crew: One
Wingspan: 40 ft (12 m)
Length: 21 ft (6 m)
Engine: 12 hp inline
Maximum speed: 30 mph
(48 km/h)

▲ The brothers tested their wing sections and
model aircraft in a homemade wind tunnel
constructed from wood with a fan at one end.
By doing this, they could see how the designs
would react under real-life conditions.

◀ The brothers
tossed a coin and
Wilbur won the
chance to be pilot.
He messed it up, so
it was Orville who
flew into the record
books. Although the
aircraft had simple
controls, the pilot
needed a lot of skill
to fly the machine
in a straight line.

▲ Orville and Wilbur traveled through
Europe and America demonstrating their
machine. The longest flight they made
lasted for just over 38 minutes.

BLERIOT TYPE XI

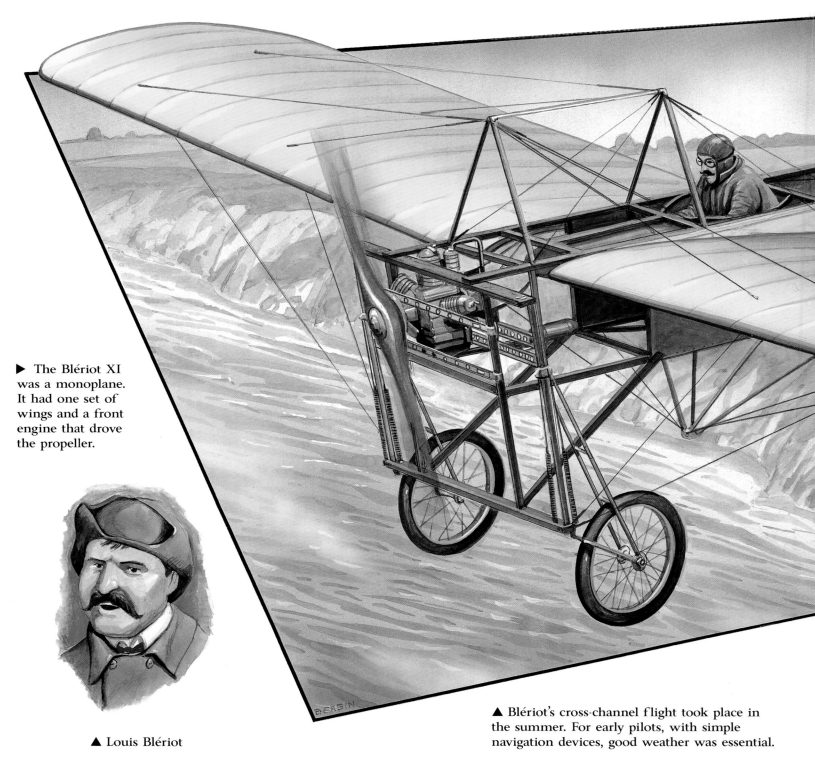

▶ The Blériot XI was a monoplane. It had one set of wings and a front engine that drove the propeller.

▲ Louis Blériot

▲ Blériot's cross-channel flight took place in the summer. For early pilots, with simple navigation devices, good weather was essential.

Almost as soon as airplanes were invented, pioneer pilots started trying to achieve flying records and meet challenges. One of the most famous was the Frenchman, Louis Blériot.

Engineer Blériot took up a newspaper challenge to fly 26 miles (41 km) over the English Channel between France and England. It seems a short distance now, but for early planes it was a dangerous touch-and-go journey. Blériot

took off from France early in the morning of July 25, 1909. Through great piloting skills and lots of luck, he landed in Britain 37 minutes later and became a flying hero. He also won a prize of £1,000 – then a huge amount of money.

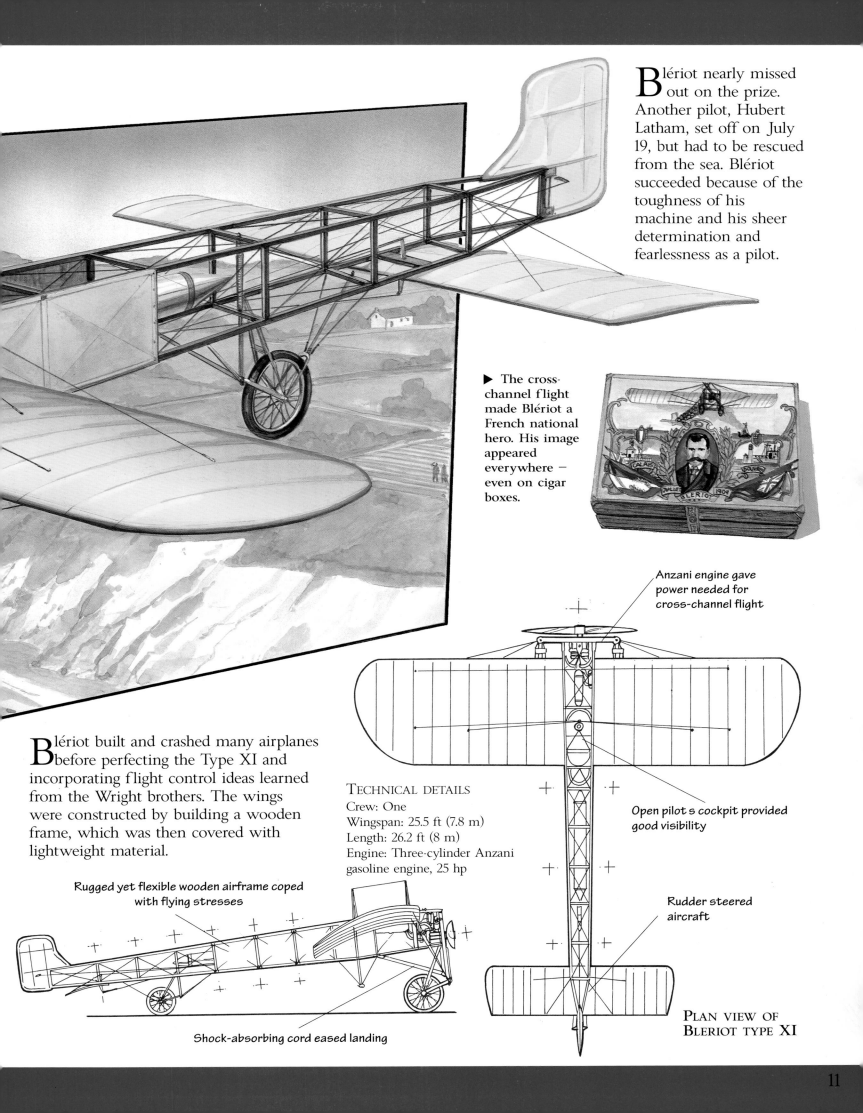

Blériot nearly missed out on the prize. Another pilot, Hubert Latham, set off on July 19, but had to be rescued from the sea. Blériot succeeded because of the toughness of his machine and his sheer determination and fearlessness as a pilot.

▶ The cross-channel flight made Blériot a French national hero. His image appeared everywhere — even on cigar boxes.

Anzani engine gave power needed for cross-channel flight

Open pilot's cockpit provided good visibility

Rudder steered aircraft

Blériot built and crashed many airplanes before perfecting the Type XI and incorporating flight control ideas learned from the Wright brothers. The wings were constructed by building a wooden frame, which was then covered with lightweight material.

TECHNICAL DETAILS
Crew: One
Wingspan: 25.5 ft (7.8 m)
Length: 26.2 ft (8 m)
Engine: Three-cylinder Anzani gasoline engine, 25 hp

Rugged yet flexible wooden airframe coped with flying stresses

Shock-absorbing cord eased landing

PLAN VIEW OF
BLERIOT TYPE XI

FOKKER D.VII

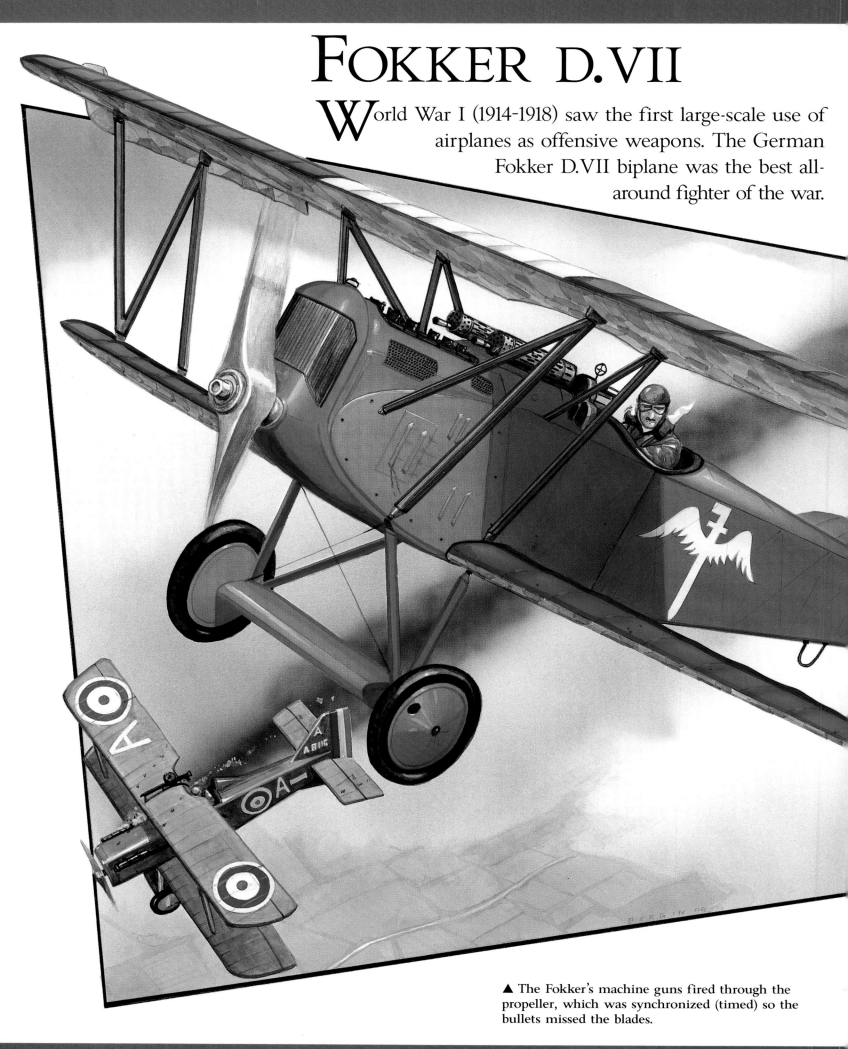

World War I (1914-1918) saw the first large-scale use of airplanes as offensive weapons. The German Fokker D.VII biplane was the best all-around fighter of the war.

▲ The Fokker's machine guns fired through the propeller, which was synchronized (timed) so the bullets missed the blades.

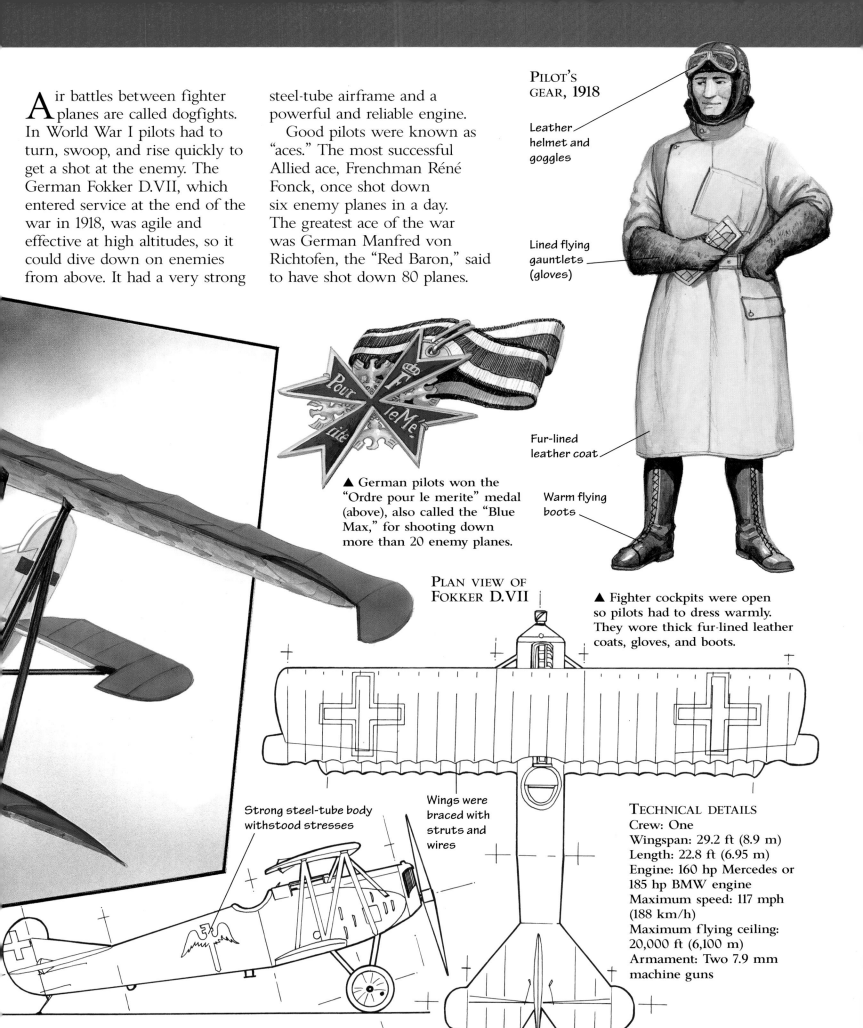

Air battles between fighter planes are called dogfights. In World War I pilots had to turn, swoop, and rise quickly to get a shot at the enemy. The German Fokker D.VII, which entered service at the end of the war in 1918, was agile and effective at high altitudes, so it could dive down on enemies from above. It had a very strong steel-tube airframe and a powerful and reliable engine.

Good pilots were known as "aces." The most successful Allied ace, Frenchman Réné Fonck, once shot down six enemy planes in a day. The greatest ace of the war was German Manfred von Richtofen, the "Red Baron," said to have shot down 80 planes.

Leather helmet and goggles

Lined flying gauntlets (gloves)

Fur-lined leather coat

Warm flying boots

▲ German pilots won the "Ordre pour le merite" medal (above), also called the "Blue Max," for shooting down more than 20 enemy planes.

PLAN VIEW OF FOKKER D.VII

▲ Fighter cockpits were open so pilots had to dress warmly. They wore thick fur-lined leather coats, gloves, and boots.

Strong steel-tube body withstood stresses

Wings were braced with struts and wires

TECHNICAL DETAILS
Crew: One
Wingspan: 29.2 ft (8.9 m)
Length: 22.8 ft (6.95 m)
Engine: 160 hp Mercedes or 185 hp BMW engine
Maximum speed: 117 mph (188 km/h)
Maximum flying ceiling: 20,000 ft (6,100 m)
Armament: Two 7.9 mm machine guns

VICKERS VIMY

Long-distance flight became the next big challenge for pilots. Once again a British newspaper put up a big prize, this time £10,000 for the first pilots to fly across the Atlantic. Two British test pilots, Captain John Alcock and Lieutenant Arthur Whitten-Brown, won the money in 1919 when they flew 1,980 miles (3,186 km) from Canada to Ireland in an adapted Vickers Vimy bomber.

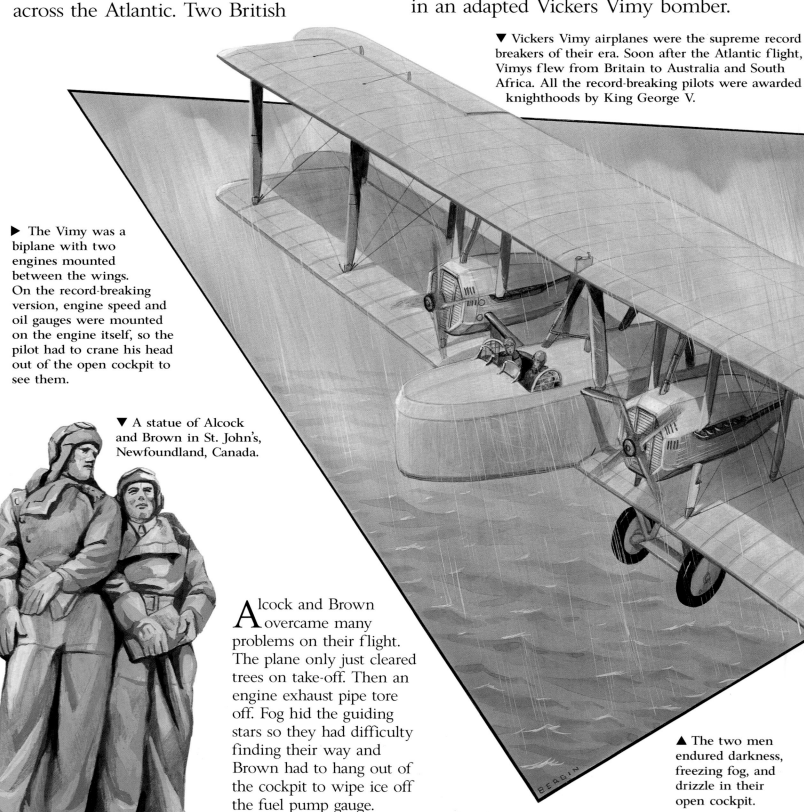

▼ Vickers Vimy airplanes were the supreme record breakers of their era. Soon after the Atlantic flight, Vimys flew from Britain to Australia and South Africa. All the record-breaking pilots were awarded knighthoods by King George V.

▶ The Vimy was a biplane with two engines mounted between the wings. On the record-breaking version, engine speed and oil gauges were mounted on the engine itself, so the pilot had to crane his head out of the open cockpit to see them.

▼ A statue of Alcock and Brown in St. John's, Newfoundland, Canada.

Alcock and Brown overcame many problems on their flight. The plane only just cleared trees on take-off. Then an engine exhaust pipe tore off. Fog hid the guiding stars so they had difficulty finding their way and Brown had to hang out of the cockpit to wipe ice off the fuel pump gauge.

▲ The two men endured darkness, freezing fog, and drizzle in their open cockpit.

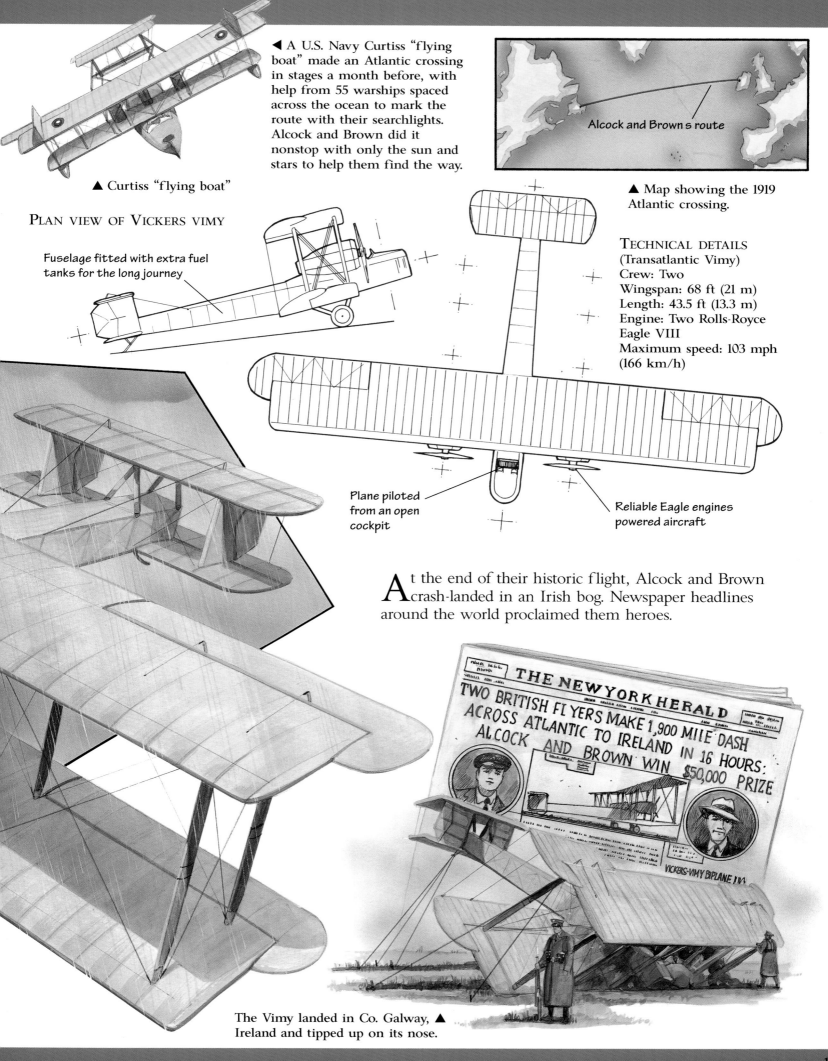

◀ A U.S. Navy Curtiss "flying boat" made an Atlantic crossing in stages a month before, with help from 55 warships spaced across the ocean to mark the route with their searchlights. Alcock and Brown did it nonstop with only the sun and stars to help them find the way.

▲ Curtiss "flying boat"

PLAN VIEW OF VICKERS VIMY

Fuselage fitted with extra fuel tanks for the long journey

Alcock and Brown's route

▲ Map showing the 1919 Atlantic crossing.

TECHNICAL DETAILS
(Transatlantic Vimy)
Crew: Two
Wingspan: 68 ft (21 m)
Length: 43.5 ft (13.3 m)
Engine: Two Rolls-Royce Eagle VIII
Maximum speed: 103 mph (166 km/h)

Plane piloted from an open cockpit

Reliable Eagle engines powered aircraft

At the end of their historic flight, Alcock and Brown crash-landed in an Irish bog. Newspaper headlines around the world proclaimed them heroes.

THE NEW YORK HERALD

TWO BRITISH FLYERS MAKE 1,900 MILE DASH ACROSS ATLANTIC TO IRELAND IN 16 HOURS: ALCOCK AND BROWN WIN $50,000 PRIZE

VICKERS-VIMY BIPLANE IVA

The Vimy landed in Co. Galway, ▲ Ireland and tipped up on its nose.

SPIRIT OF ST. LOUIS

Although the public was very impressed by the achievements of the Vickers Vimy pilots, it took a tough journey by one determined man to finally convince people that flying was reliable. In May 1927 Charles Lindbergh set off from a rain-soaked New York field in his little airplane *Spirit of St. Louis* to attempt the first solo flight of the Atlantic. More than 33 hours and 3,610 miles (5,810 km) later he landed in northern France.

Charles ▲
Lindbergh

PLAN VIEW OF *SPIRIT OF ST. LOUIS*

Struts braced and strengthened wings

Lindbergh was a fascinating but controversial man. He had been a stunt pilot and a U.S. mail pilot before his solo flight won him $25,000. Overnight he became the most famous flier in the world. The spotlight of publicity was on him for the rest of his eventful life, especially a few years later when his baby son was kidnapped and never found.

TECHNICAL DETAILS
Crew: One
Wingspan: 46 ft (14 m)
Length: 27.8 ft (8.4 m)
Engine: 237-hp Wright J-5C Whirlwind
Cruise speed: 105 mph (169 km/h)

Lindbergh's flight was fraught with danger. His main problem was tiredness. He became so exhausted he began to see ghostly figures and hear voices. At one point he confused sea and sky and almost flew into the waves.

◀ Lindbergh had to keep checking the wing struts of his aircraft to make sure that they didn't ice up.

When Lindbergh landed his airplane a cheering mob nearly tore it apart to get souvenirs. French police had to rescue both plane and exhausted pilot from the crush.

◄ The plane was a modified version of a Ryan M-2 monoplane, its wings braced by struts. The design was chosen to minimize drag (air resistance) on the journey. The Ryan also had a reliable economical engine.

Its fuel tanks were placed in front of the cockpit with the result that Lindbergh couldn't see ahead. To overcome this, Lindbergh had a retractable periscope fitted to the cockpit.

◄ The aircraft's navigation aids were very basic. Finding the way relied on the skill of the pilot.

▼ Lindbergh was hoisted high on the shoulders of the French crowd.

Charles Lindbergh's feat marked an important turning point in aviation. His flight pointed the way toward safe, long-distance air travel.

SUPERMARINE S.6B

An exciting contest, the Schneider Trophy, was held in the 1920s and 1930s between seaplanes from different countries. Britain won the trophy with the fast, sleek Supermarine S.6B.

The S.6B had several design features that helped make it a record breaker. It was a monoplane, so it created less drag in the air than a biplane. It had a streamlined metal structure. Above all it had a very powerful supercharged engine. This meant the engine had a blower that squeezed as much air as possible into the combustion chambers. Here it was ignited with fuel to develop the power that turned the propeller around, driving the plane through the air.

Experience with the S.6B engine led to the Rolls-Royce Merlin engine that powered Allied aircraft during World War II (1939-1945).

▲ In 1931 Royal Air Force Flight Lieutenant George Stainforth set a new speed record of 408 mph (655 km/h). Flying at such high speeds meant that the airplane shook, making it hard to control. To stop this, the designers fitted parts of the aircraft with balance weights to keep them stable.

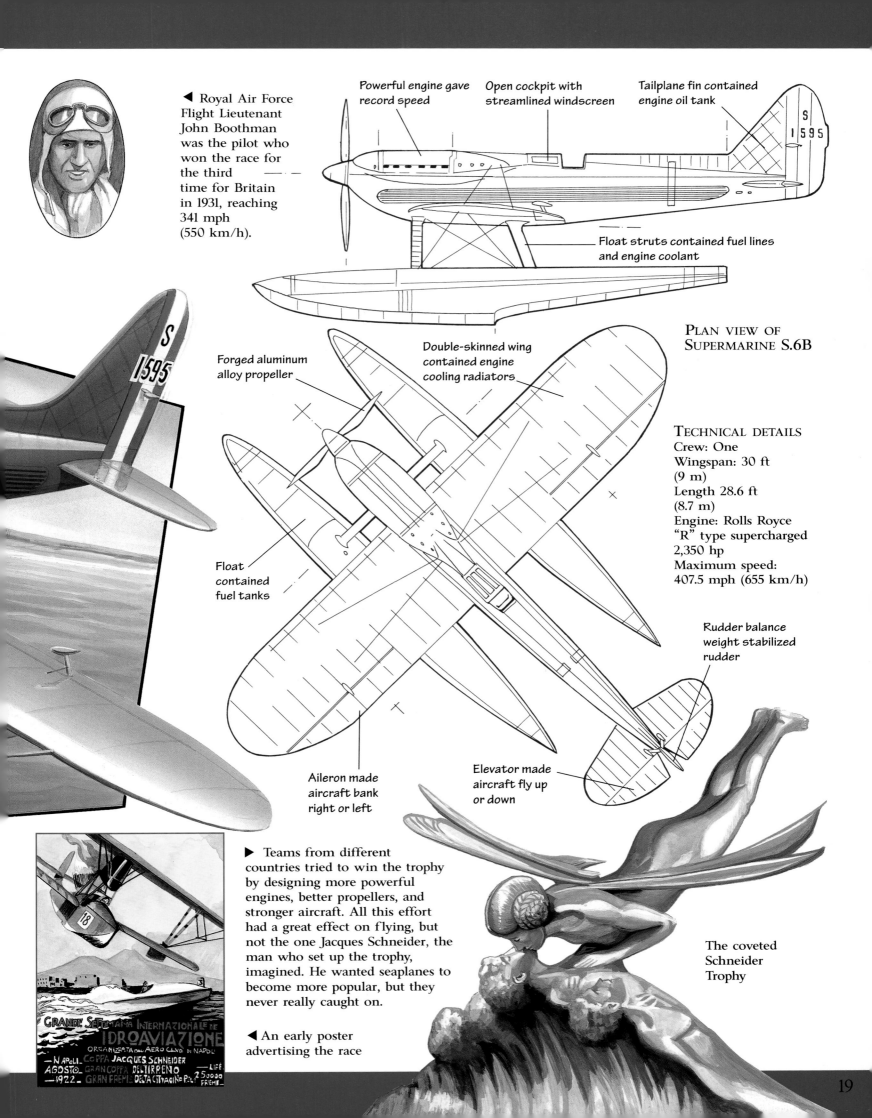

◀ Royal Air Force Flight Lieutenant John Boothman was the pilot who won the race for the third time for Britain in 1931, reaching 341 mph (550 km/h).

Powerful engine gave record speed

Open cockpit with streamlined windscreen

Tailplane fin contained engine oil tank

S 1595

Float struts contained fuel lines and engine coolant

PLAN VIEW OF SUPERMARINE S.6B

Forged aluminum alloy propeller

Double-skinned wing contained engine cooling radiators

TECHNICAL DETAILS
Crew: One
Wingspan: 30 ft (9 m)
Length 28.6 ft (8.7 m)
Engine: Rolls Royce "R" type supercharged 2,350 hp
Maximum speed: 407.5 mph (655 km/h)

Float contained fuel tanks

Rudder balance weight stabilized rudder

Aileron made aircraft bank right or left

Elevator made aircraft fly up or down

S 1595

▶ Teams from different countries tried to win the trophy by designing more powerful engines, better propellers, and stronger aircraft. All this effort had a great effect on flying, but not the one Jacques Schneider, the man who set up the trophy, imagined. He wanted seaplanes to become more popular, but they never really caught on.

The coveted Schneider Trophy

◀ An early poster advertising the race

GRANDE SETTIMANA INTERNAZIONALE DE
IDROAVIAZIONE
ORGANIZZATA DAL AERO CLVB DI NAPOLI
N APOLI COPPA JACQUES SCHNEIDER
AGOSTO GRAN COPPA DEL TIRRENO LIRE
1922 GRAN PREMIO DELLA CITTA DI NAPOLI 250.000 PREMII

LANCASTER NIGHT BOMBER

Military aircraft played a vital part in World War II (1939-1945), none more famously than the specially modified British Lancaster night bombers of the Royal Air Force's 617 Squadron, later nicknamed the "Dambusters."

On the night of May 16, 1943, 19 Lancasters set out to destroy the Ruhr dams that produced hydroelectric power for German factories. The Dambusters used a daring secret weapon, a "bouncing bomb" designed by engineer Sir Barnes Wallis.

▶ The bold night raid left one dam breached and others damaged.

The bomb had to be released at exactly 60 ft (18 m) above the water. Each plane had two lights with beams that met exactly 60 ft beneath the fuselage so the bomb aimer could work out how high the aircraft was. The plane had to fly at 250 mph (400 km/h) and drop the bomb at exactly the right distance from the dam. After bouncing to the dam, the bomb sank. At 30 ft (9 m) down, water pressure triggered the explosion.

HOW IT WORKED

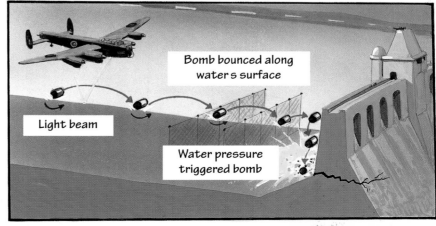

Bomb bounced along water's surface

Light beam

Water pressure triggered bomb

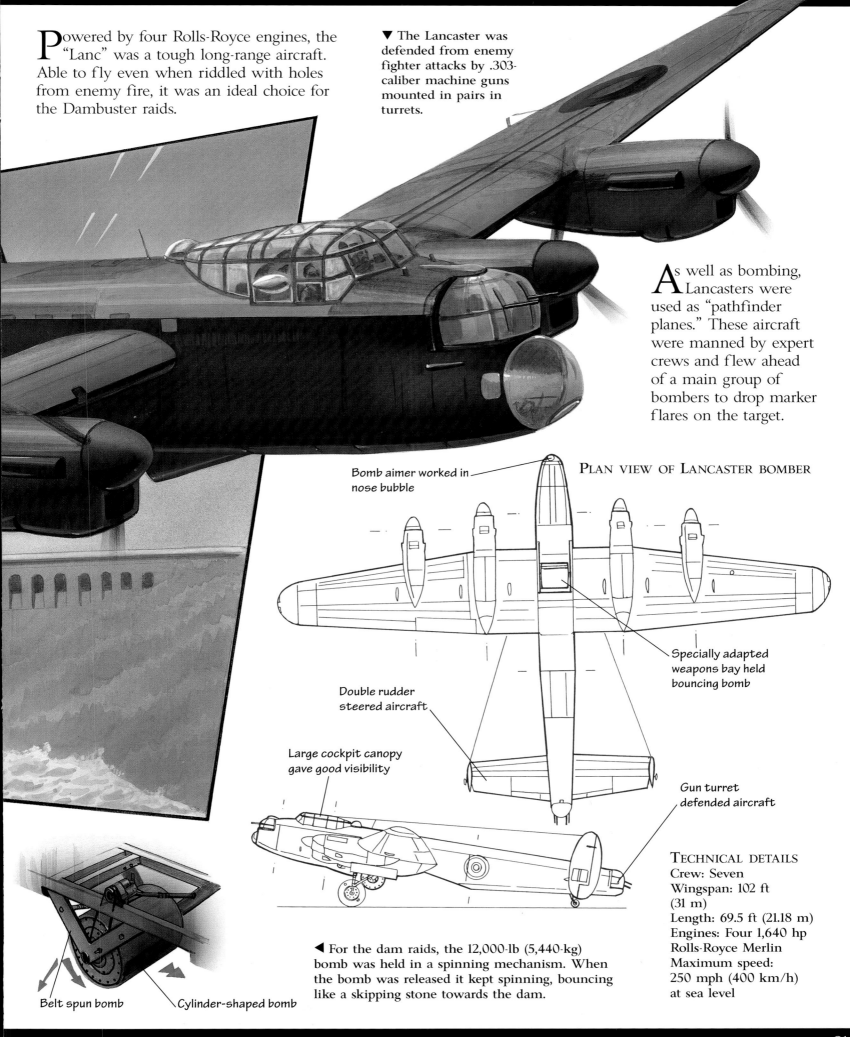

Powered by four Rolls-Royce engines, the "Lanc" was a tough long-range aircraft. Able to fly even when riddled with holes from enemy fire, it was an ideal choice for the Dambuster raids.

▼ The Lancaster was defended from enemy fighter attacks by .303-caliber machine guns mounted in pairs in turrets.

As well as bombing, Lancasters were used as "pathfinder planes." These aircraft were manned by expert crews and flew ahead of a main group of bombers to drop marker flares on the target.

PLAN VIEW OF LANCASTER BOMBER

Bomb aimer worked in nose bubble

Specially adapted weapons bay held bouncing bomb

Double rudder steered aircraft

Large cockpit canopy gave good visibility

Gun turret defended aircraft

TECHNICAL DETAILS
Crew: Seven
Wingspan: 102 ft (31 m)
Length: 69.5 ft (21.18 m)
Engines: Four 1,640 hp Rolls-Royce Merlin
Maximum speed: 250 mph (400 km/h) at sea level

◄ For the dam raids, the 12,000-lb (5,440-kg) bomb was held in a spinning mechanism. When the bomb was released it kept spinning, bouncing like a skipping stone towards the dam.

Belt spun bomb

Cylinder-shaped bomb

P-51D MUSTANG

The American P-51D Mustang was the best all-around fighter of World War II. Its main job was to escort U.S. bombers on daylight raids over enemy territory, protecting them from attack by enemy fighters.

▲ World War II fighter pilots often decorated their aircraft with nose art.

▲ Colonel Joe Mason of the 352nd Fighter Group escorts a group of B-17 bombers of the U.S. Eighth Air Force in 1943.

Mustangs were fitted with long-range fuel tanks under the wings as well as internal fuel tanks on the wings. That meant they could travel long distances with the bombers, jettisoning the long-range tanks when empty. They could fly higher than any other fighter in 1940 and they were very fast because they had a powerful Rolls-Royce Merlin engine and a streamlined body. Mustangs had a "laminar flow" wing design. This means that the wings had a special cross-section shape that cut down on drag as the plane traveled through the air. This wing design also helped the aircraft's high-speed performance, making it a formidable dogfighter.

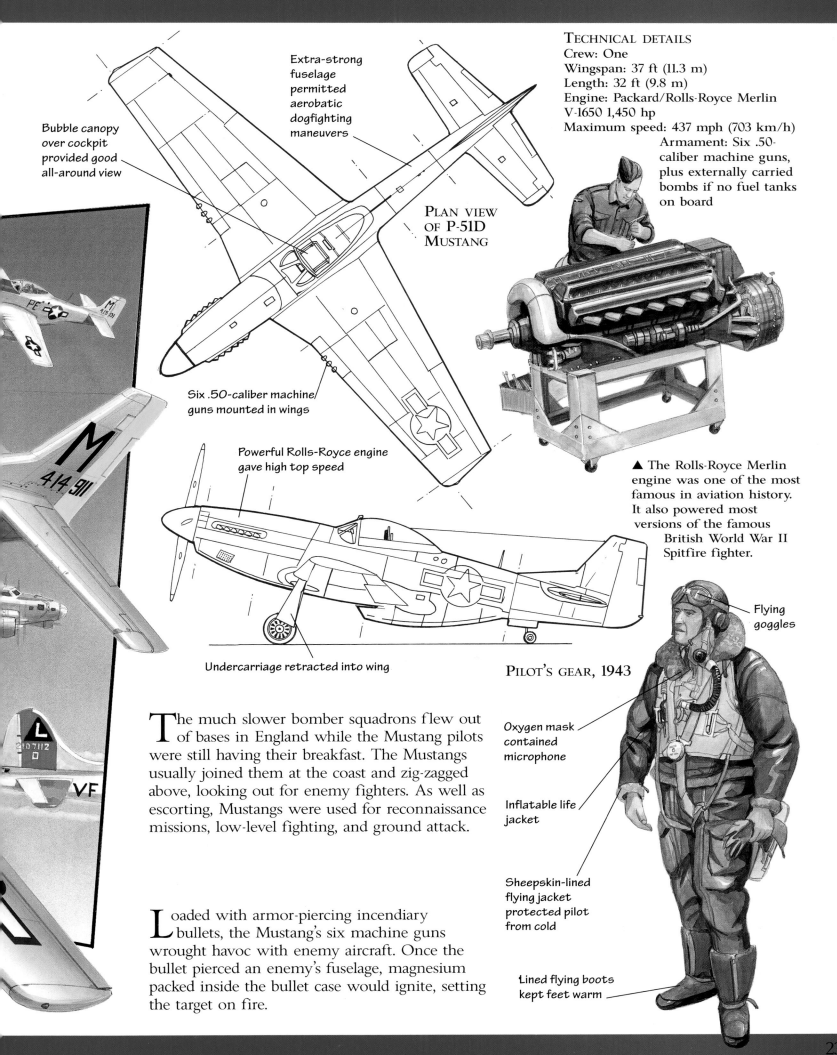

Bubble canopy over cockpit provided good all-around view

Extra-strong fuselage permitted aerobatic dogfighting maneuvers

TECHNICAL DETAILS
Crew: One
Wingspan: 37 ft (11.3 m)
Length: 32 ft (9.8 m)
Engine: Packard/Rolls-Royce Merlin V-1650 1,450 hp
Maximum speed: 437 mph (703 km/h)
Armament: Six .50-caliber machine guns, plus externally carried bombs if no fuel tanks on board

PLAN VIEW OF P-51D MUSTANG

Six .50-caliber machine guns mounted in wings

Powerful Rolls-Royce engine gave high top speed

▲ The Rolls-Royce Merlin engine was one of the most famous in aviation history. It also powered most versions of the famous British World War II Spitfire fighter.

Undercarriage retracted into wing

PILOT'S GEAR, 1943

Flying goggles

Oxygen mask contained microphone

Inflatable life jacket

Sheepskin-lined flying jacket protected pilot from cold

Lined flying boots kept feet warm

The much slower bomber squadrons flew out of bases in England while the Mustang pilots were still having their breakfast. The Mustangs usually joined them at the coast and zig-zagged above, looking out for enemy fighters. As well as escorting, Mustangs were used for reconnaissance missions, low-level fighting, and ground attack.

Loaded with armor-piercing incendiary bullets, the Mustang's six machine guns wrought havoc with enemy aircraft. Once the bullet pierced an enemy's fuselage, magnesium packed inside the bullet case would ignite, setting the target on fire.

MESSERSCHMITT ME 262

During World War II both sides raced to develop a jet engine. The German Messerschmitt Me 262-1a was the first jet aircraft to enter the war, in 1944. It was used to bomb ground forces or to attack enemy bombers. Despite its superiority in the air it didn't change the course of the war because not enough were made.

▼ In a jet engine, air gets sucked in at the front. It goes through a compressor (a series of metal vanes) that squeezes as much air as possible into a combustion chamber. Here the air is mixed with fuel and ignited, creating hot gases that roar out of the exhaust nozzle at high speed, powering the plane forward.

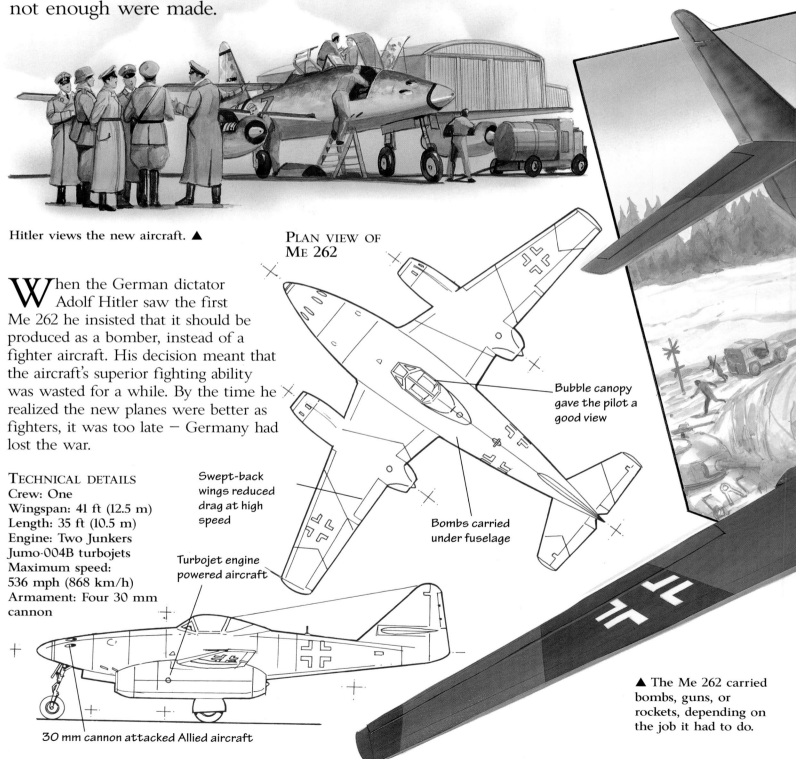

Hitler views the new aircraft. ▲

PLAN VIEW OF ME 262

When the German dictator Adolf Hitler saw the first Me 262 he insisted that it should be produced as a bomber, instead of a fighter aircraft. His decision meant that the aircraft's superior fighting ability was wasted for a while. By the time he realized the new planes were better as fighters, it was too late – Germany had lost the war.

TECHNICAL DETAILS
Crew: One
Wingspan: 41 ft (12.5 m)
Length: 35 ft (10.5 m)
Engine: Two Junkers Jumo-004B turbojets
Maximum speed: 536 mph (868 km/h)
Armament: Four 30 mm cannon

Swept-back wings reduced drag at high speed

Bubble canopy gave the pilot a good view

Bombs carried under fuselage

Turbojet engine powered aircraft

30 mm cannon attacked Allied aircraft

▲ The Me 262 carried bombs, guns, or rockets, depending on the job it had to do.

Heinkel 178

▶ German research work on jet engines was carried out by the engineer Pabst von Ohain. In 1939 his Heinkel 178 became the first plane to fly powered solely by a jet engine. For the Allies Sir Frank Whittle designed his own turbojet engine, which went into the first RAF fighter, the Gloster Meteor.

◀ Although the aircraft was fast, the brand new jet-engine technology was very unreliable, and many Me 262s were lost through crashes.

◀ The Me 262's jet engines made it more powerful than any enemy fighter, and it could fire rockets into the back of an Allied bomber while staying well out of range of the craft's tail gunners.

▲ In the picture above, an Me 262 attacks U.S. troops during the Battle of the Bulge of 1944.

DE HAVILLAND COMET

After World War II airplanes began to fill the skies, led by the Comet, the first ever jet-powered airliner. It entered service in 1952, reducing long-distance flying times by up to half. Suddenly it was possible to travel across the world in just hours, but the journeys became hazardous when Comets began to crash. The work that British engineers did to find the reasons for the crashes helped to make future airliners safer.

▲ The Comet prototype made its first historic flight in 1949 with famous test pilot John Cunningham at the controls.

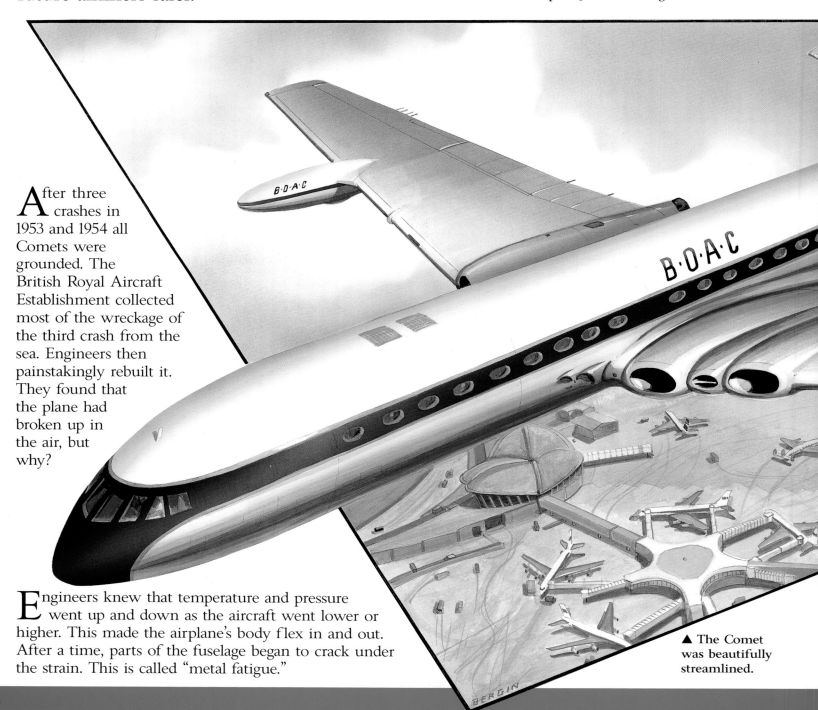

After three crashes in 1953 and 1954 all Comets were grounded. The British Royal Aircraft Establishment collected most of the wreckage of the third crash from the sea. Engineers then painstakingly rebuilt it. They found that the plane had broken up in the air, but why?

Engineers knew that temperature and pressure went up and down as the aircraft went lower or higher. This made the airplane's body flex in and out. After a time, parts of the fuselage began to crack under the strain. This is called "metal fatigue."

▲ The Comet was beautifully streamlined.

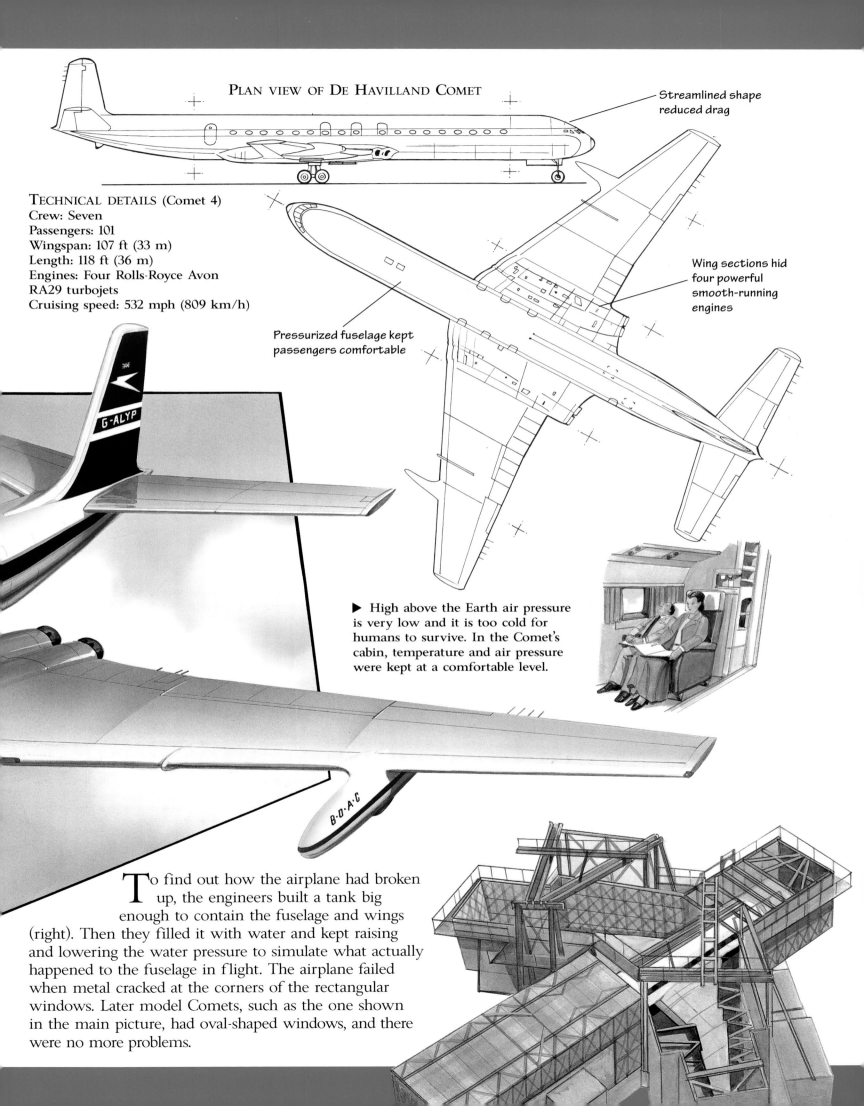

PLAN VIEW OF DE HAVILLAND COMET

Streamlined shape
reduced drag

TECHNICAL DETAILS (Comet 4)
Crew: Seven
Passengers: 101
Wingspan: 107 ft (33 m)
Length: 118 ft (36 m)
Engines: Four Rolls-Royce Avon
RA29 turbojets
Cruising speed: 532 mph (809 km/h)

Wing sections hid
four powerful
smooth-running
engines

Pressurized fuselage kept
passengers comfortable

G-ALYP

▶ High above the Earth air pressure
is very low and it is too cold for
humans to survive. In the Comet's
cabin, temperature and air pressure
were kept at a comfortable level.

B·O·A·C

To find out how the airplane had broken
up, the engineers built a tank big
enough to contain the fuselage and wings
(right). Then they filled it with water and kept raising
and lowering the water pressure to simulate what actually
happened to the fuselage in flight. The airplane failed
when metal cracked at the corners of the rectangular
windows. Later model Comets, such as the one shown
in the main picture, had oval-shaped windows, and there
were no more problems.

HARRIER JUMP JET

I n the late 1960s the Harrier Jump Jet first appeared, manufactured by the British Hawker company. It excited and amazed the flying world with a new trick, vertical take-off and landing (VTOL for short).

H arriers can take off straight upward, hover stationary in the air, and land in a very small space. These unique features make them ideal as warplanes on aircraft carriers, although on board ship they usually get airborne using a short take-off run (a method called STOL – short take-off and landing). Harriers carry bombs or attack enemy planes with heat-seeking air-to-air missiles.

M oveable engine nozzles are the secret of the Harrier's success. When they point backward, engine gases blast out through them to thrust the plane forward. However, they can also swivel to direct the jet blast downward, so the plane can hover, rise up, or sink gently down.

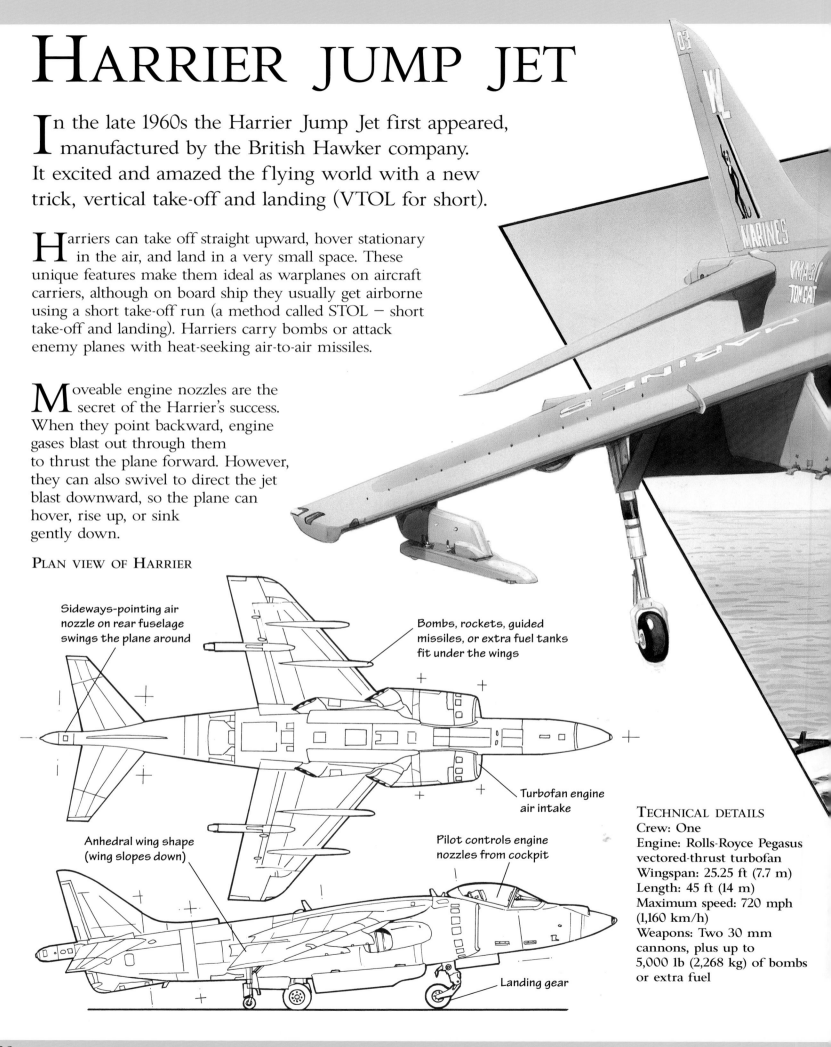

PLAN VIEW OF HARRIER

Sideways-pointing air nozzle on rear fuselage swings the plane around

Bombs, rockets, guided missiles, or extra fuel tanks fit under the wings

Turbofan engine air intake

Anhedral wing shape (wing slopes down)

Pilot controls engine nozzles from cockpit

Landing gear

TECHNICAL DETAILS
Crew: One
Engine: Rolls-Royce Pegasus vectored-thrust turbofan
Wingspan: 25.25 ft (7.7 m)
Length: 45 ft (14 m)
Maximum speed: 720 mph (1,160 km/h)
Weapons: Two 30 mm cannons, plus up to 5,000 lb (2,268 kg) of bombs or extra fuel

▲ Harrier mission patch of the U.S. Marine Corps.

◄ Air forces and navies use Harriers. Sea Harriers operate from aircraft carriers of the Royal Navy and the U.S. Marine Corps.

The Harrier's Rolls-Royce Pegasus engine is a powerplant type known as a turbofan. It gets its name because at the front it has a big fan. As the fan spins, it sucks in lots of air. Some of the air is ejected through the front two nozzles. The rest is fed through a compressor into a combustion chamber where it gets mixed with fuel and ignited.

Engine exhaust nozzle

Turbofan blades

▶ The Harrier's Pegasus engine can be removed for maintenance.

SR-71 BLACKBIRD

A superspy of the air from the 1960s to the 1980s, the Lockheed SR-71 Blackbird flew higher than any other aircraft, almost into space, and was unbelievably fast. Such extremes helped it to stay hidden as the crew took detailed secret pictures of hostile territory. The arrow-like SR-71 got its nickname because it was painted blue-black.

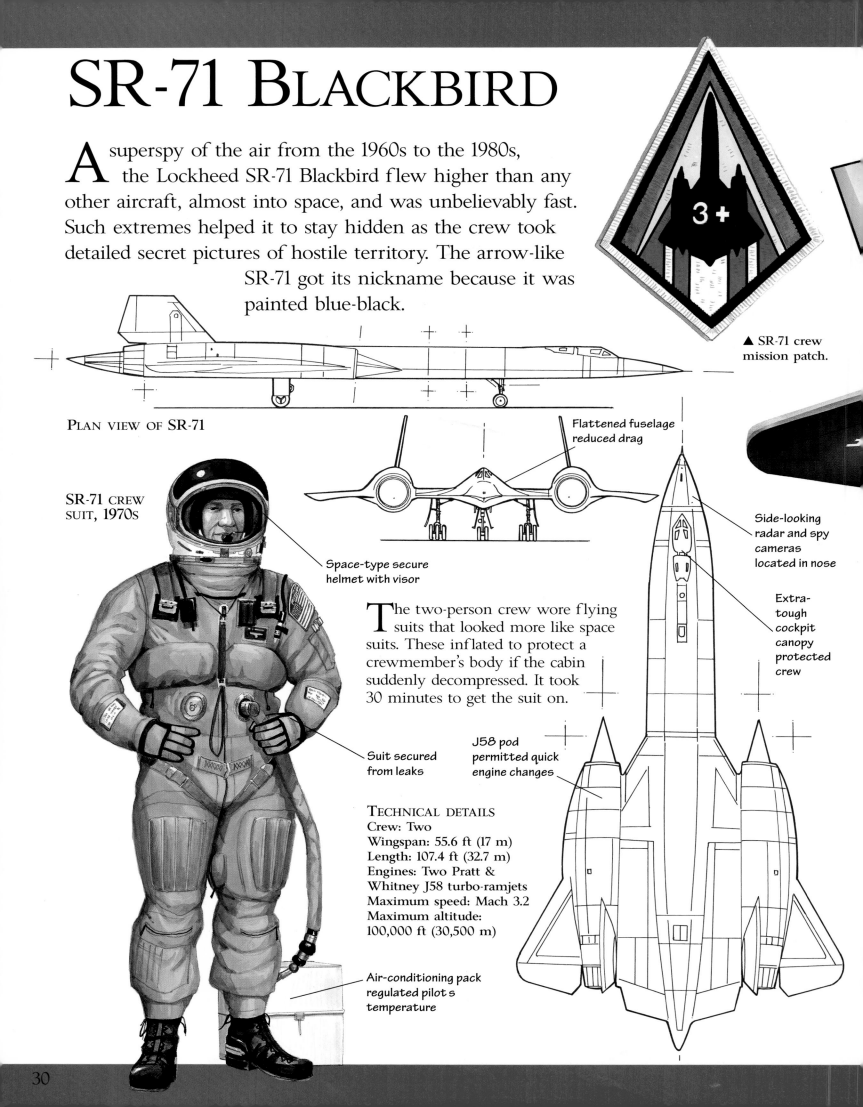

▲ SR-71 crew mission patch.

PLAN VIEW OF SR-71

SR-71 CREW SUIT, 1970S

Flattened fuselage reduced drag

Space-type secure helmet with visor

The two-person crew wore flying suits that looked more like space suits. These inflated to protect a crewmember's body if the cabin suddenly decompressed. It took 30 minutes to get the suit on.

Side-looking radar and spy cameras located in nose

Extra-tough cockpit canopy protected crew

Suit secured from leaks

J58 pod permitted quick engine changes

TECHNICAL DETAILS
Crew: Two
Wingspan: 55.6 ft (17 m)
Length: 107.4 ft (32.7 m)
Engines: Two Pratt & Whitney J58 turbo-ramjets
Maximum speed: Mach 3.2
Maximum altitude: 100,000 ft (30,500 m)

Air-conditioning pack regulated pilot's temperature

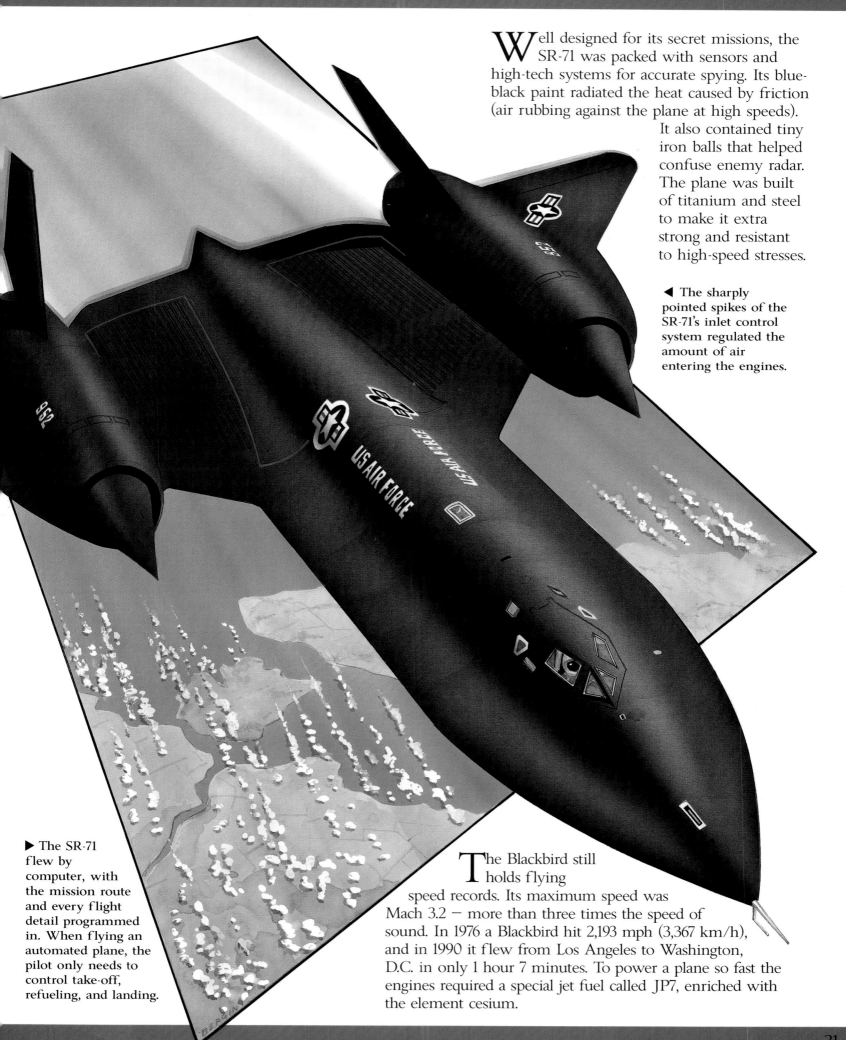

Well designed for its secret missions, the SR-71 was packed with sensors and high-tech systems for accurate spying. Its blue-black paint radiated the heat caused by friction (air rubbing against the plane at high speeds). It also contained tiny iron balls that helped confuse enemy radar. The plane was built of titanium and steel to make it extra strong and resistant to high-speed stresses.

◀ The sharply pointed spikes of the SR-71's inlet control system regulated the amount of air entering the engines.

▶ The SR-71 flew by computer, with the mission route and every flight detail programmed in. When flying an automated plane, the pilot only needs to control take-off, refueling, and landing.

The Blackbird still holds flying speed records. Its maximum speed was Mach 3.2 — more than three times the speed of sound. In 1976 a Blackbird hit 2,193 mph (3,367 km/h), and in 1990 it flew from Los Angeles to Washington, D.C. in only 1 hour 7 minutes. To power a plane so fast the engines required a special jet fuel called JP7, enriched with the element cesium.

BOEING 747

O n February 7, 1969, a test crew flew a huge new flying machine, the Boeing 747, for the first time. It had a new "wide-bodied" design, with space inside to carry hundreds of passengers plus cargo. It swiftly earned the nickname "jumbo jet," with a tail as high as a six-storey building, a wing area bigger than a basketball court, and a fuselage twice the length of the Wright Brothers' first flight.

T he 747 became the most influential airliner of all time. It could carry hundreds more people than any previous jet, and revolutionized air transport by making long-haul flights available to everyone. The aircraft has three decks. The flight deck is in the top section. The middle section is for passengers and the bottom section for cargo. There's room for more than 500 passengers on modern jumbos. Different versions of the 747 have been in use all over the world.

▶ The main picture shows the first prototype 747 to fly, in 1969. Airlines who ordered jumbos from Boeing had their logos painted on the fuselage. The very first jumbo in passenger service was Pan Am's N732PA.

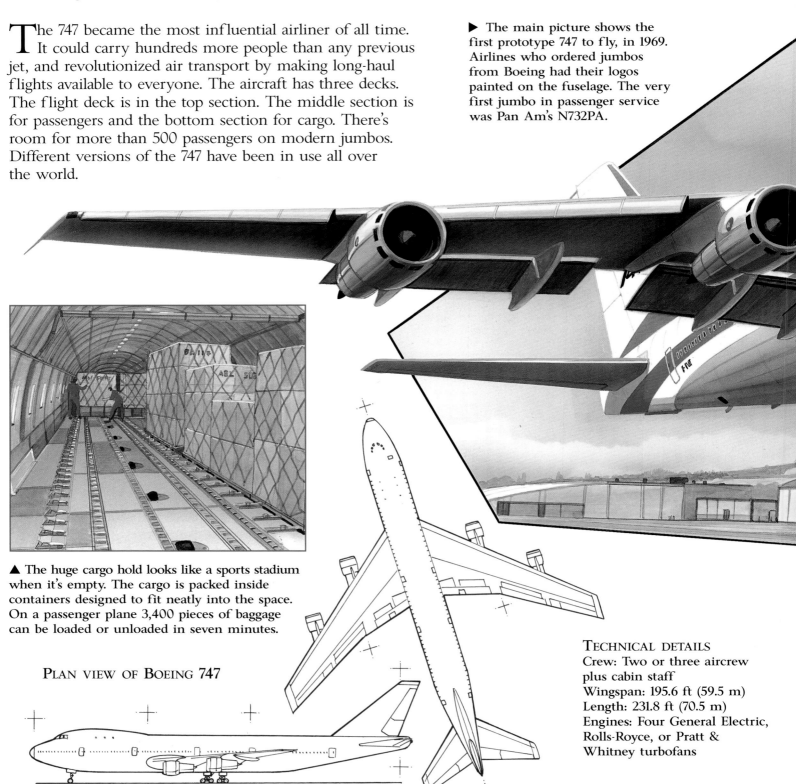

▲ The huge cargo hold looks like a sports stadium when it's empty. The cargo is packed inside containers designed to fit neatly into the space. On a passenger plane 3,400 pieces of baggage can be loaded or unloaded in seven minutes.

PLAN VIEW OF BOEING 747

TECHNICAL DETAILS
Crew: Two or three aircrew plus cabin staff
Wingspan: 195.6 ft (59.5 m)
Length: 231.8 ft (70.5 m)
Engines: Four General Electric, Rolls-Royce, or Pratt & Whitney turbofans

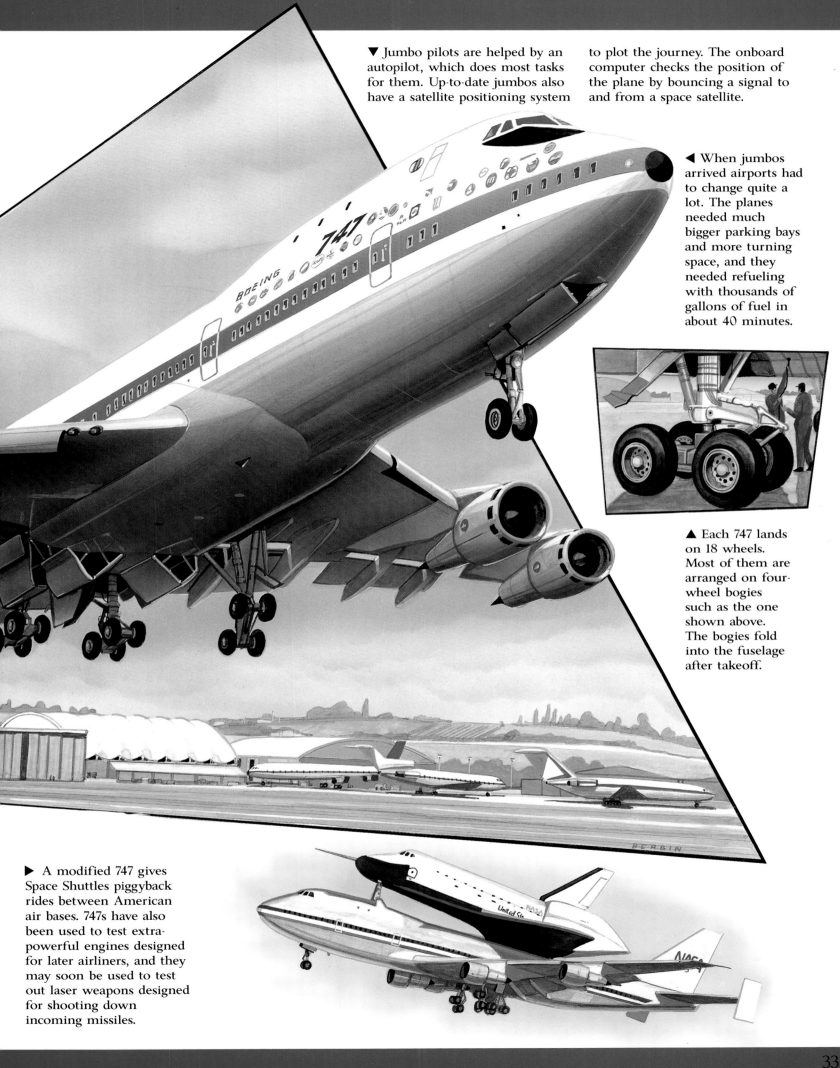

▼ Jumbo pilots are helped by an autopilot, which does most tasks for them. Up-to-date jumbos also have a satellite positioning system to plot the journey. The onboard computer checks the position of the plane by bouncing a signal to and from a space satellite.

◄ When jumbos arrived airports had to change quite a lot. The planes needed much bigger parking bays and more turning space, and they needed refueling with thousands of gallons of fuel in about 40 minutes.

▲ Each 747 lands on 18 wheels. Most of them are arranged on four-wheel bogies such as the one shown above. The bogies fold into the fuselage after takeoff.

► A modified 747 gives Space Shuttles piggyback rides between American air bases. 747s have also been used to test extra-powerful engines designed for later airliners, and they may soon be used to test out laser weapons designed for shooting down incoming missiles.

CONCORDE

In 1969 the Aerospatiale/British Aerospace Concorde became the first passenger airliner to go supersonic, which means traveling faster than the speed of sound. With a cruising speed of Mach 2 (1,350 mph or 2,172.5 km/h) it is faster than many rifle bullets and covers two miles (4.42 km) every 2.75 seconds at a cruising altitude twice as high as Mount Everest.

Concorde's elegant streamlined body is designed for speed rather than for big loads of cargo or passengers. It travels from London to New York in less than four hours. Because the aircraft crosses time zones, passengers arrive in New York more than an hour earlier than when they left London! It's an expensive way to travel, so the high-paying passengers are given luxury treatment on their super-fast journey.

▲ Filled with dials and switches, the cockpit of Concorde looks decidedly different when compared to those of modern airliners, with their ranks of video screens.

Concorde's delta wing shape provides lift for the aircraft. They also carry the engines and lots of fuel tanks. Fuel is automatically transferred back and forth between tanks during a flight to alter the weight balance of the plane, keeping it at the correct angle in the air.

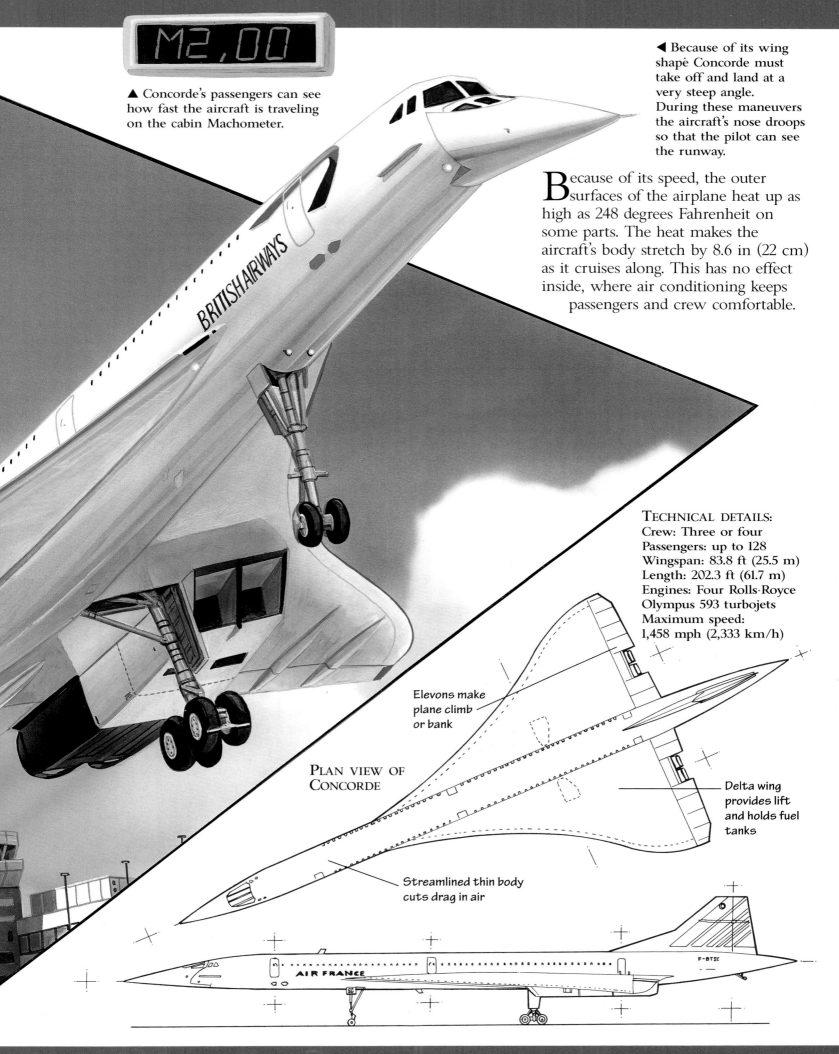

M2,00

▲ Concorde's passengers can see how fast the aircraft is traveling on the cabin Machometer.

◀ Because of its wing shape Concorde must take off and land at a very steep angle. During these maneuvers the aircraft's nose droops so that the pilot can see the runway.

Because of its speed, the outer surfaces of the airplane heat up as high as 248 degrees Fahrenheit on some parts. The heat makes the aircraft's body stretch by 8.6 in (22 cm) as it cruises along. This has no effect inside, where air conditioning keeps passengers and crew comfortable.

BRITISH AIRWAYS

TECHNICAL DETAILS:
Crew: Three or four
Passengers: up to 128
Wingspan: 83.8 ft (25.5 m)
Length: 202.3 ft (61.7 m)
Engines: Four Rolls-Royce
Olympus 593 turbojets
Maximum speed:
1,458 mph (2,333 km/h)

Elevons make plane climb or bank

Delta wing provides lift and holds fuel tanks

PLAN VIEW OF CONCORDE

Streamlined thin body cuts drag in air

AIR FRANCE

F-16 FIGHTING FALCON

▲ The USAF "Thunderbirds" F-16 Air Display team in action.

In 1979 the F-16, a super-agile fighter bomber, came into service with the U.S. Air Force. It could make breathtaking aerobatic moves, pushing both plane and pilot to their limits. It was equipped with new hi-tech gear that soon became standard on most military jet aircraft. Updated F-16s are still in use today.

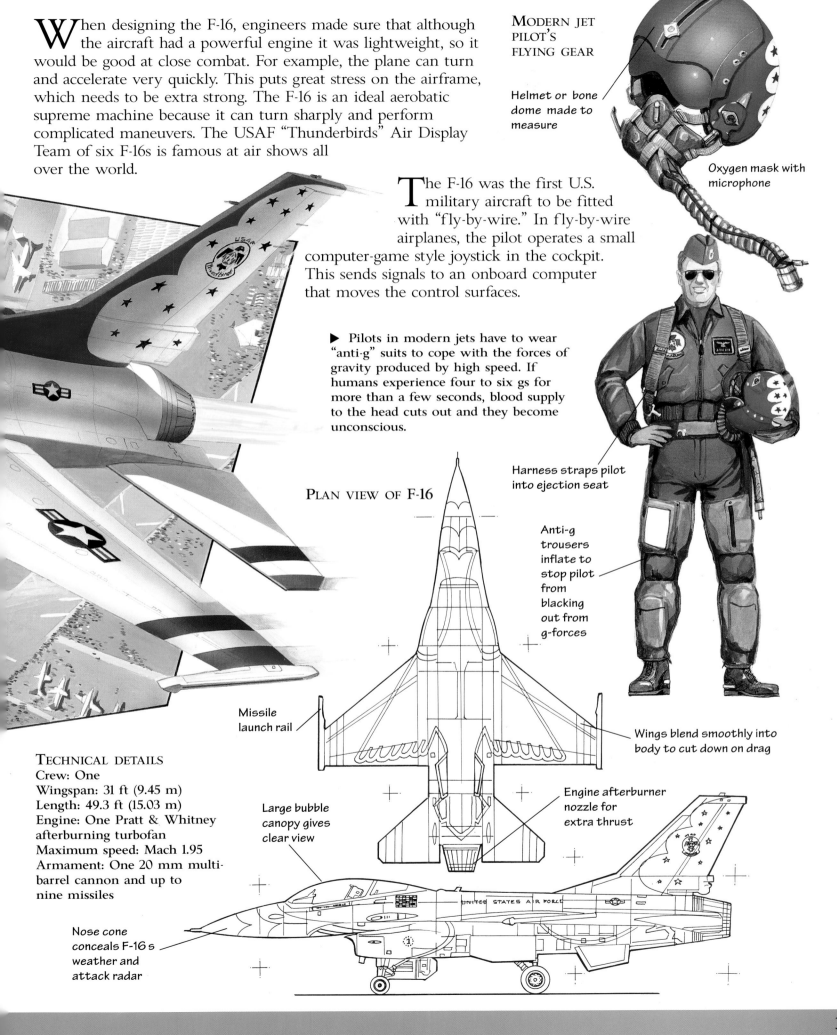

When designing the F-16, engineers made sure that although the aircraft had a powerful engine it was lightweight, so it would be good at close combat. For example, the plane can turn and accelerate very quickly. This puts great stress on the airframe, which needs to be extra strong. The F-16 is an ideal aerobatic supreme machine because it can turn sharply and perform complicated maneuvers. The USAF "Thunderbirds" Air Display Team of six F-16s is famous at air shows all over the world.

MODERN JET PILOT'S FLYING GEAR

Helmet or bone dome made to measure

Oxygen mask with microphone

The F-16 was the first U.S. military aircraft to be fitted with "fly-by-wire." In fly-by-wire airplanes, the pilot operates a small computer-game style joystick in the cockpit. This sends signals to an onboard computer that moves the control surfaces.

▶ Pilots in modern jets have to wear "anti-g" suits to cope with the forces of gravity produced by high speed. If humans experience four to six gs for more than a few seconds, blood supply to the head cuts out and they become unconscious.

Harness straps pilot into ejection seat

Anti-g trousers inflate to stop pilot from blacking out from g-forces

PLAN VIEW OF F-16

Missile launch rail

Wings blend smoothly into body to cut down on drag

Engine afterburner nozzle for extra thrust

TECHNICAL DETAILS
Crew: One
Wingspan: 31 ft (9.45 m)
Length: 49.3 ft (15.03 m)
Engine: One Pratt & Whitney afterburning turbofan
Maximum speed: Mach 1.95
Armament: One 20 mm multi-barrel cannon and up to nine missiles

Large bubble canopy gives clear view

Nose cone conceals F-16's weather and attack radar

F-117 STEALTH FIGHTER

If you wanted to destroy an enemy aircraft you would use radar to find it and heat-seeking missiles to shoot it down. But what if the plane was invisible? Welcome to the hi-tech world of the U.S. F-117 Stealth jet fighter. Its faceted shape and black coloring are instantly recognizable, but the enemy wouldn't even see it coming because the plane is designed not to emit traceable signals. Now Stealth technology is being incorporated into future warplane designs.

▲ Stealth squadron mission patch.

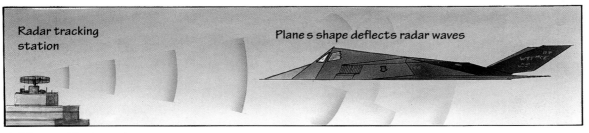

Radar tracking station

Plane's shape deflects radar waves

▲ The F-117's shape breaks up radar waves. The flat underside only reflects signals back when the aircraft is directly above, and radar tends to be "blind" when a target is overhead.

PLAN VIEW OF F-117 STEALTH FIGHTER

Angled nose

Ailerons control direction of aircraft

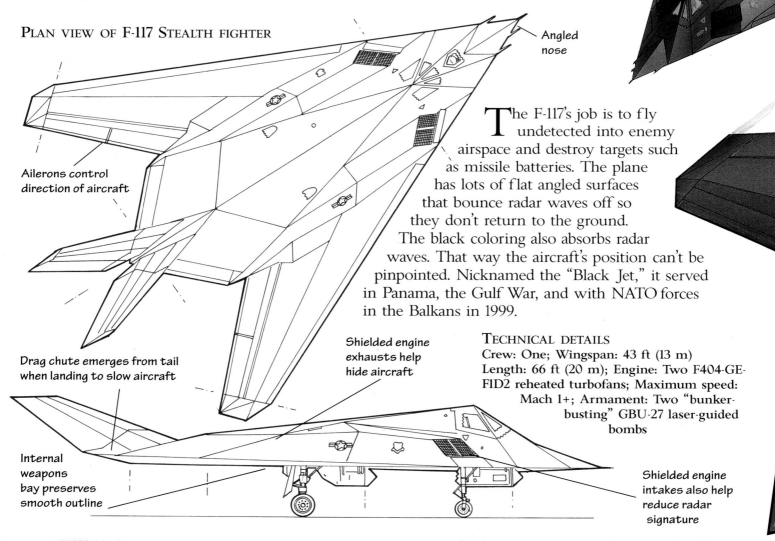

The F-117's job is to fly undetected into enemy airspace and destroy targets such as missile batteries. The plane has lots of flat angled surfaces that bounce radar waves off so they don't return to the ground. The black coloring also absorbs radar waves. That way the aircraft's position can't be pinpointed. Nicknamed the "Black Jet," it served in Panama, the Gulf War, and with NATO forces in the Balkans in 1999.

Drag chute emerges from tail when landing to slow aircraft

Shielded engine exhausts help hide aircraft

TECHNICAL DETAILS
Crew: One; Wingspan: 43 ft (13 m)
Length: 66 ft (20 m); Engine: Two F404-GE-F1D2 reheated turbofans; Maximum speed: Mach 1+; Armament: Two "bunker-busting" GBU-27 laser-guided bombs

Internal weapons bay preserves smooth outline

Shielded engine intakes also help reduce radar signature

BERGIN

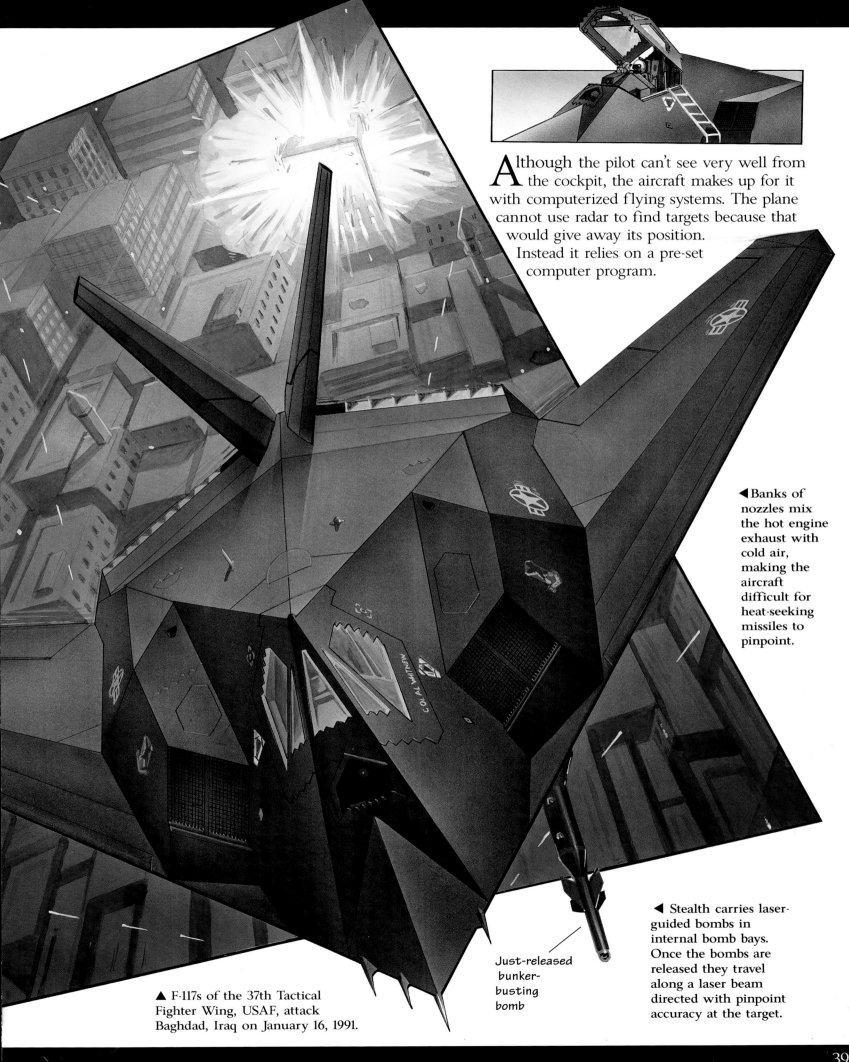

Although the pilot can't see very well from the cockpit, the aircraft makes up for it with computerized flying systems. The plane cannot use radar to find targets because that would give away its position. Instead it relies on a pre-set computer program.

◀Banks of nozzles mix the hot engine exhaust with cold air, making the aircraft difficult for heat-seeking missiles to pinpoint.

◀ Stealth carries laser-guided bombs in internal bomb bays. Once the bombs are released they travel along a laser beam directed with pinpoint accuracy at the target.

Just-released bunker-busting bomb

▲ F-117s of the 37th Tactical Fighter Wing, USAF, attack Baghdad, Iraq on January 16, 1991.

GEAR AND GADGETS

Airplane design is changing all the time and so are the gadgets that pilots have on board to help them. Military pilots need equipment that gives them a high-tech advantage over the enemy. Airline pilots need equipment to help them fly their planes safely and without delays. What a big difference from the early days of flight, when pilots navigated by the stars like ancient sailors!

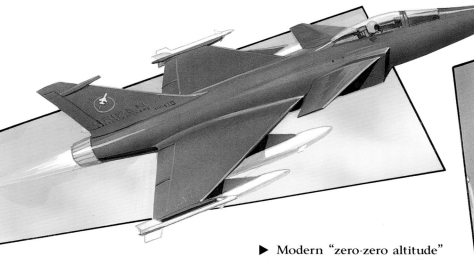

▲ Many modern fighters have ECM onboard. The initials stand for "electronic counter-measures," equipment that jams enemy radar signals. The Swedish Saab Viggen fighter carries pods of ECM equipment under its wings.

▶ Modern "zero-zero altitude" ejector seats can save a military pilot even when the plane is going at very low speed or is very near the ground. Once a pilot works the ejector seat control the cockpit canopy blows off and the pilot shoots upwards at high speed, well away from the plane, in a rocket-propelled seat.

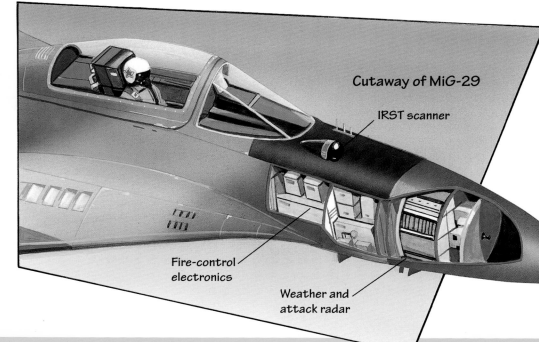

Cutaway of MiG-29

IRST scanner

Fire-control electronics

Weather and attack radar

◀ When a fighter aircraft uses radar to search for a target it gives its own position away to the enemy. The Russian MiG-29 has a "magic eye" to solve the problem. Inside the ball-shaped eye a mirror revolves, silently scanning the sky for infra-red heat (called a "thermal signature") given out by other planes. It is called an IRST (infra-red search and track) device. It is connected to the "fire-control" system of the aircraft - the parts that aim and fire the weapons.

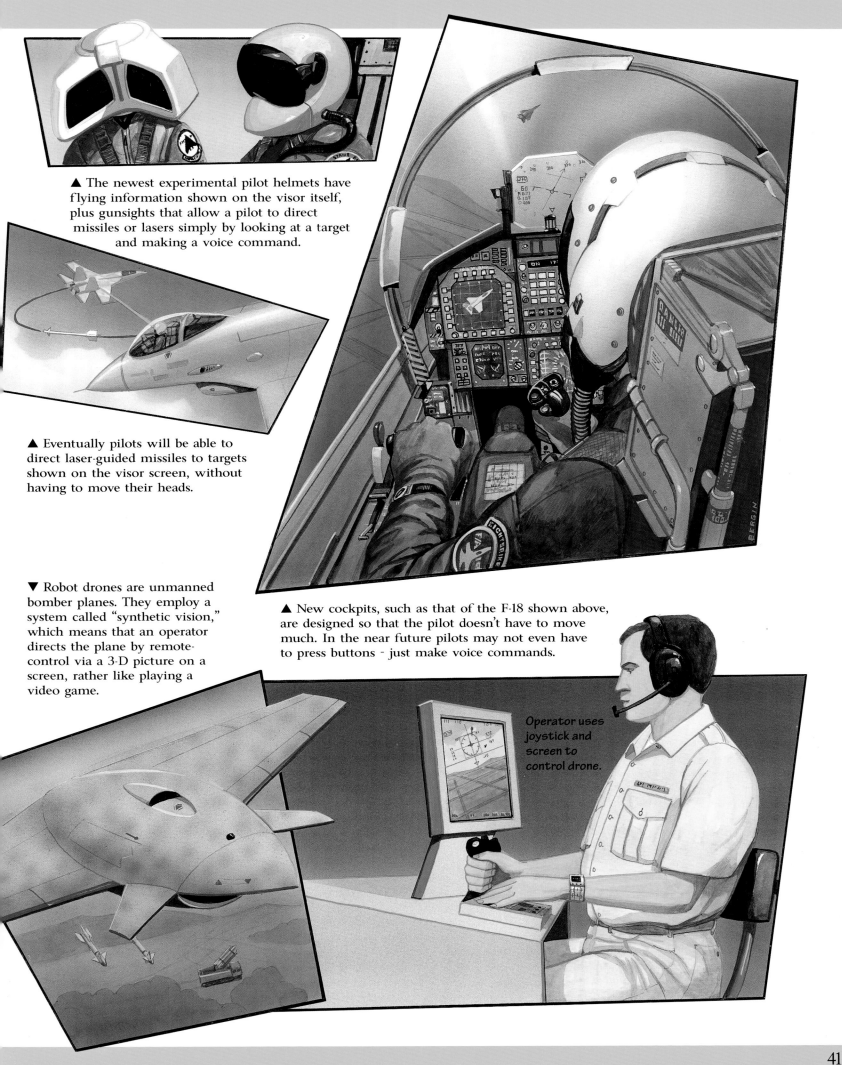

▲ The newest experimental pilot helmets have flying information shown on the visor itself, plus gunsights that allow a pilot to direct missiles or lasers simply by looking at a target and making a voice command.

▲ Eventually pilots will be able to direct laser-guided missiles to targets shown on the visor screen, without having to move their heads.

▼ Robot drones are unmanned bomber planes. They employ a system called "synthetic vision," which means that an operator directs the plane by remote-control via a 3-D picture on a screen, rather like playing a video game.

▲ New cockpits, such as that of the F-18 shown above, are designed so that the pilot doesn't have to move much. In the near future pilots may not even have to press buttons - just make voice commands.

Operator uses joystick and screen to control drone.

NEW DIRECTIONS

Future fighters will probably have some Stealth features to confuse the enemy, such as lots of body angles and a radar-absorbing skin. However, unlike Stealth they'll be able to do amazing aerobatic tricks in the air and they'll be able to take part in "digital dogfights," firing missiles from far away without ever seeing an enemy plane. Civil airliners will probably be even bigger than Jumbos, and they'll be able to fly through any weather.

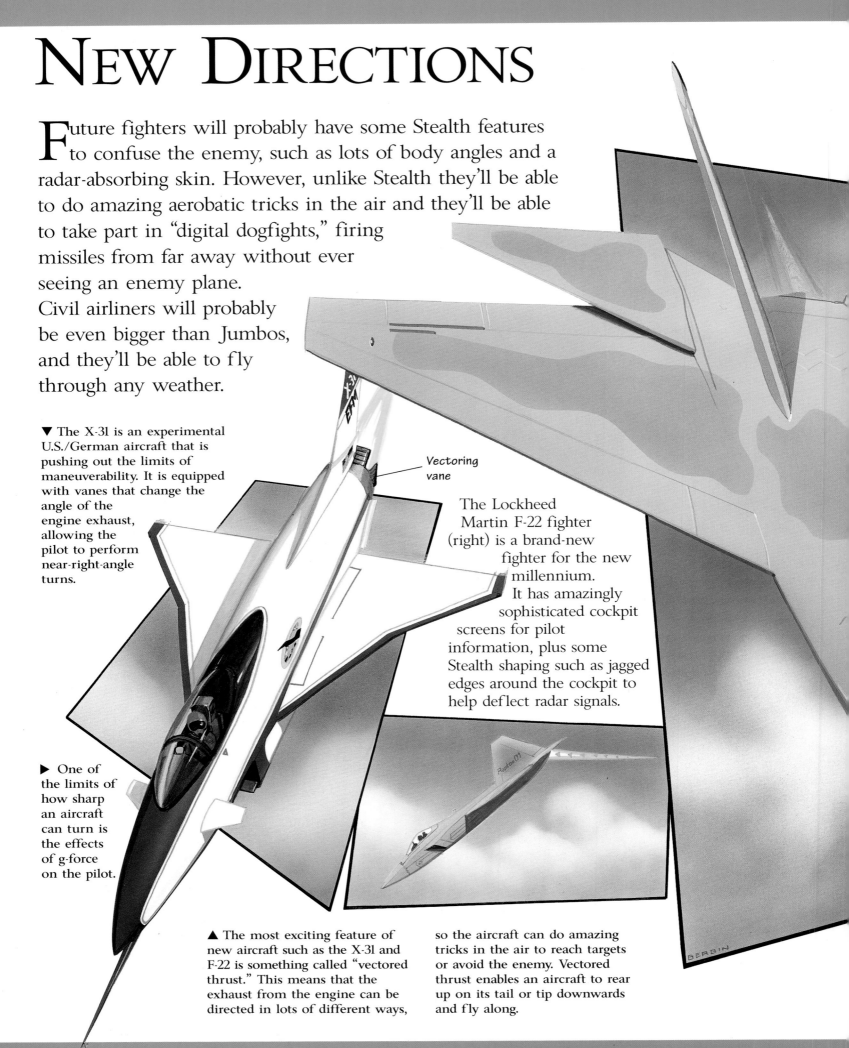

▼ The X-3l is an experimental U.S./German aircraft that is pushing out the limits of maneuverability. It is equipped with vanes that change the angle of the engine exhaust, allowing the pilot to perform near-right-angle turns.

Vectoring vane

The Lockheed Martin F-22 fighter (right) is a brand-new fighter for the new millennium. It has amazingly sophisticated cockpit screens for pilot information, plus some Stealth shaping such as jagged edges around the cockpit to help deflect radar signals.

▶ One of the limits of how sharp an aircraft can turn is the effects of g-force on the pilot.

▲ The most exciting feature of new aircraft such as the X-3l and F-22 is something called "vectored thrust." This means that the exhaust from the engine can be directed in lots of different ways, so the aircraft can do amazing tricks in the air to reach targets or avoid the enemy. Vectored thrust enables an aircraft to rear up on its tail or tip downwards and fly along.

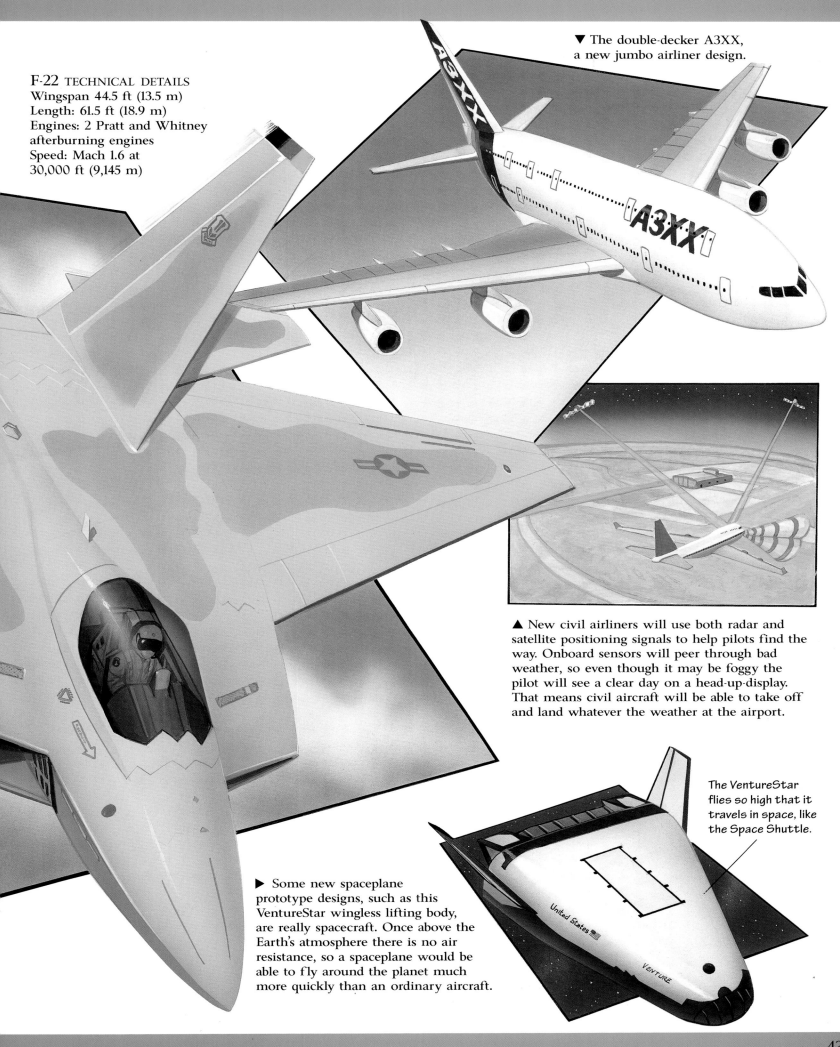

F-22 TECHNICAL DETAILS
Wingspan 44.5 ft (13.5 m)
Length: 61.5 ft (18.9 m)
Engines: 2 Pratt and Whitney
afterburning engines
Speed: Mach 1.6 at
30,000 ft (9,145 m)

▼ The double-decker A3XX,
a new jumbo airliner design.

A3XX

▲ New civil airliners will use both radar and
satellite positioning signals to help pilots find the
way. Onboard sensors will peer through bad
weather, so even though it may be foggy the
pilot will see a clear day on a head-up-display.
That means civil aircraft will be able to take off
and land whatever the weather at the airport.

The VentureStar
flies so high that it
travels in space, like
the Space Shuttle.

► Some new spaceplane
prototype designs, such as this
VentureStar wingless lifting body,
are really spacecraft. Once above the
Earth's atmosphere there is no air
resistance, so a spaceplane would be
able to fly around the planet much
more quickly than an ordinary aircraft.

United States

VENTURE

GLOSSARY

Ailerons: Moveable parts on aircraft wings. They can be moved automatically to roll the craft to left or right and alter its position in the air.

Airframe: The main body of an aircraft (not its engines).

Altimeter: A cockpit instrument for measuring the height of an aircraft in the sky.

Anti-g suit: A flying suit with sections that inflate to regulate a jet pilot's blood flow.

Biplane: An aircraft with two sets of wings, one above the other.

Bomb bay: A bomb-holding compartment beneath an airplane's fuselage.

Bracing wires: Strong connecting wires between sets of wings on vintage aircraft.

Bubble canopy: The see-through cockpit lid on many modern jets.

Combustion chamber: A chamber inside an engine where fuel and air are mixed and burned.

Delta wing: A triangle-shaped wing that helps reduce drag (air resistance) at high speeds.

Dogfight: An air battle between two fighter aircraft.

ECM: Initials standing for electronic counter-measures – equipment that can jam enemy radar signals.

Elevators: Moveable surfaces on an aircraft's tail. They can be moved to make the aircraft dive or climb.

IRST: Initials standing for infra-red search and track, equipment that detects infra-red heat given out by objects.

Fly-by-wire: Computerized controls that automatically adjust an aircraft's position in flight.

▲ Modern flying gear

Fuselage: The central body of a plane.

HUD: Initials standing for head-up display, when information is projected onto a screen in front of a pilot.

Interrupter gun gear: A mechanism that allows a machine gun to fire between spinning propeller blades.

Jet engine: An engine in which air gets sucked in through the front and goes through a compressor that squeezes as much air as possible into the combustion chamber. There the mixture is ignited to burn and create exhaust gases.

Joystick: The main control lever in the cockpit of an aircraft.

Laser-guided bombs: Bombs that follow a laser beam directed at the target.

Mach 1: The speed of sound at a given height. Fast plane speeds are measured in Mach numbers.

Monoplane: An aircraft with only one set of wings.

Radar: Radio pulses that are transmitted through the air. They bounce off an object and return to the receiver. The position of the object can then be fixed.

Rudder: A vertical surface on the back of an aircraft's tail. It helps steer the plane.

Sensors: Electronic measuring equipment fitted to a modern aircraft, used to measure various things such as heat, speed, or air pressure. They relay the information to the aircraft's main computer system.

Stealth-shaping: Angled shapes on an aircraft's body to scatter incoming radar beams and make the plane invisible to radar tracking equipment.

STOL: Initials standing for short takeoff and landing. They mean that an aircraft can lift off the ground in a short distance.

Strut: A strong supporting bar between the wings of a vintage aircraft.

Supercharged engine: An engine with a device called a "blower" at the front to squeeze as much air into the cylinders as possible.

Supersonic: An aircraft that can go faster than the speed of sound.

Synthetic vision: A 3-D cartoon-style picture of the scene outside a plane.

Turbofan: An engine with a fan at the front, which passes extra air around the "core" engine.

Vectored thrust: Steering the angle of the exhaust jet. This can be used to perform vertical take-off in the Harrier, but in some future designs will be used to give extra maneuverability.

VTOL: Initials standing for vertical takeoff and landing. They mean that an aircraft can lift up vertically from the ground.

Wingspan: The measurement from one wingtip across to another.

Wing warping: Cords that twisted the edges of the wings to steer the earliest aircraft.

▶ The Harrier's Pegasus engine

TIMELINE

1891-96 German Otto Lilienthal experiments with gliders, paving the way for manned flight.

1903 The Wright Brothers complete the world's first powered, controlled manned flight, with Orville Wright at the controls of the Wright *Flyer I* at Kitty Hawk, North Carolina.

1906 The first airplane flight in Europe, by Alberto Santos-Dumont in his aircraft *14 bis*.

1907-8 Frenchman Paul Cornu builds the world's first working helicopter.

1909 Frenchman Louis Blériot becomes the first pilot to fly the English Channel in a Blériot XI.

1910 The world's first regular air passenger service flies between two U.S. cities.

1912 The first flight in an aircraft with an enclosed cabin for the pilot.

1914-18 World War I. Aircraft used in battle for the first time. Fighter "aces" battle it out one-to-one in airborne dogfights.

1918 The German Fokker D.VII fighter plane enters service. It proves to be the best all-around fighter of the war.

1919 Captain John Alcock and Lieutenant Arthur Whitten-Brown become the first pilots to fly across the Atlantic, in a Vickers Vimy biplane.

1920s Aircraft first carry air mail.

1927 Charles Lindbergh completes the first solo flight of the Atlantic in his aircraft *Spirit of St. Louis*.

1931 British Royal Air Force Flight Lieutenant John Boothman wins the Schneider Trophy outright in a Supermarine S.6B seaplane.

1932 Amelia Earhart becomes the first woman to fly the Atlantic alone and nonstop.

1937 In Britain, Frank Whittle tests W.U., the world's first jet engine.

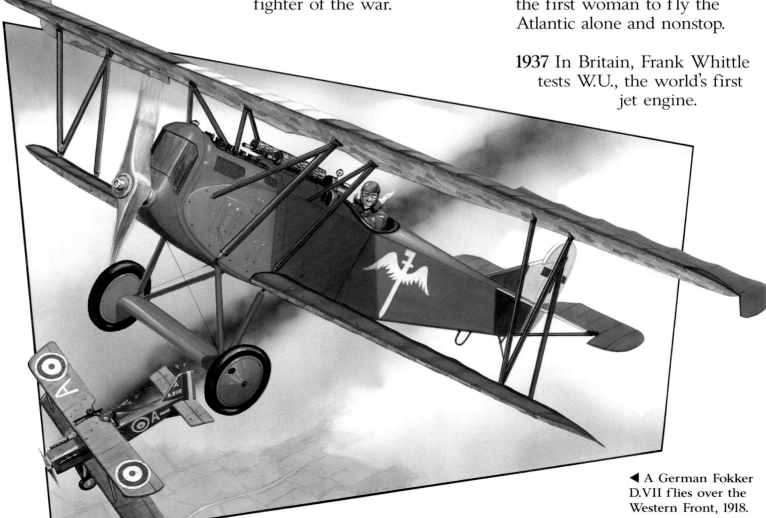

◀ A German Fokker D.VII flies over the Western Front, 1918.

1939 The German Heinkel He 178 completes the world's first jet aircraft flight.

1939-45 World War II. Aircraft are vital to the outcome of the conflict. The P-51D Mustang proves to be the best all-around fighter aircraft of the war.

1943 Avro Lancaster night bombers take part in the famous Dambuster raid on German dams in the Ruhr valley.

1944 The Messerschmitt Me 262-1a is the first jet fighter to be used in war.

1947 Chuck Yeager becomes the first pilot to fly supersonic, in a Bell X-1 rocket plane.

▲ A Lockheed SR-71 takes spy photographs, 1970s.

1952 The De Havilland DH 106 Comet reduces long-distance passenger-carrying flight times by half. It heralds the growth of mass air travel. The aircraft is grounded after crashes, but an improved model later enters service.

1963 The Hawker Siddeley P1127, the first experimental fighter to use the revolutionary Vertical Takeoff and Landing system, is tested on board HMS *Ark Royal*. It led to the Harrier.

1969 The first flight of the Aerospatiale/British Aerospace Concorde, the first passenger airliner to fly supersonic.

1969 The first flight of a Boeing 747 Jumbo Jet, an airliner with a new wide-bodied design to carry hundreds more passengers than ever before.

1976 The SR-71 "Blackbird" spyplane sets a new speed record for a jet aircraft. It is able to fly higher than any previous airplane.

1979 The F-16 Fighting Falcon flies for the first time. It carries hi-tech computer equipment that eventually becomes standard on military aircraft.

1983 First flight of the Lockheed F-117A Stealth jet fighter. The aircraft uses new radar-invisible design technology.

1986 Dick Rutan and Jeanna Yeager become the first people to fly around the world non-stop, in their aircraft *Voyager*.

1989 First flight of the Northrop B-2 Stealth bomber.

1999 Stealth fighters are in use by NATO forces in the Balkans.

INDEX

Acknowledgments

Franklin Watts would like to thank the following for their help in creating this book:

Leonard Butterfield and Charles Hunt for consultancy

Lynn Bresler for the index